When Making Others *Happy* Is Making You *Miserable*

HOW TO BREAK THE PATTERN OF PEOPLE PLEASING AND CONFIDENTLY LIVE YOUR LIFE

STUDY GUIDE | SIX SESSIONS

KAREN EHMAN

HarperChristian
Resources

Contents

How to Use This Guide

Group Size

The *When Making Others Happy Is Making You Miserable* video curriculum is designed to be experienced in a group setting such as a Bible study, online study group, or any small group gathering. After viewing each video together, members will participate in a group discussion and then complete the in-between sessions work.

Materials Needed

Each participant should have their own study guide, which includes video outline notes, directions for activities and discussion questions, as well as a reading plan and personal studies to deepen learning between sessions. Participants are also strongly encouraged to have a copy of the *When Making Others Happy Is Making You Miserable* book. Reading the book alongside the video curriculum provides even deeper insights that make the journey richer and more meaningful (also, a few of the questions pertain to material covered in the book).

Timing

The time notations—for example (17 minutes)—indicate the *actual* time of video segments and the *suggested* time for each activity or discussion.

For example:

Individual Activity: What Is God Asking Me to Do? (5 MINUTES)

Adhering to the suggested times will enable you to complete each session in one hour. If you have additional time, there are bonus questions listed for your group to answer, thereby expanding your group's meeting time to between an hour and fifteen minutes or an hour and a half. If you are also having refreshments and a time of sharing prayer requests, factor in another thirty minutes.

Facilitation

Each group should appoint a facilitator who is responsible for starting the video and for keeping track of time during discussions and activities. Facilitators may also read questions aloud and monitor discussions, prompting participants to respond and ensuring that everyone can participate.

Between-Sessions Personal Study

Maximize the impact of the course with additional study between group sessions. Carving out about two hours total for personal study between meeting times will enable you to complete both the book and between-session studies by the end of the course. For each session, you may wish to complete the personal study all in one sitting or to spread it out over a few days (for example, working on it a half hour a day on four different days that week). PLEASE NOTE: If you are unable to finish (or even start!) your between-sessions personal study, still attend the group study video session. We are all busy and life happens. You are still wanted and welcome at class even if you don't have your "homework" done.

Scripture Memory

Each session's study includes a key Scripture verse that highlights the topic of the session theme. If you wish to maximize your learning experience, you may attempt to memorize these verses. To assist you with this goal, all six verses are printed in the back of the study guide.

You may photocopy this page on paper or card stock and then cut the verses out. (You really creative and crafty types may even want to do a little hand lettering). Then keep them in a convenient place—perhaps your car, purse, or tote bag. You can practice memorizing them while waiting in the carpool line or at the doctor's office. Or you may wish to post them at your kitchen sink or on your bathroom mirror where you will see them each day. Laminating them will help to keep them from getting ruined if they get splashed. You may even wish to make a digital copy of them to use as a lock screen for your phone.

It may be helpful to have the group facilitator inquire if any participants are attempting to memorize the key verses. Perhaps those members will want to show up five minutes early (or stay afterward) to practice reciting them to each other.

The Prison of People Pleasing

Session One Memory Verse

"Am I now trying to win the approval of human beings, or of God?
Or am I trying to please people? If I were still trying to please people,
I would not be a servant of Christ." (Galatians 1:10)

Welcome to week one of *When Making Others Happy Is Making You Miserable.* My greatest hope and deepest prayer is that you will learn how important it is to not put people in the place of God but allow him to be the one who calls the shots in your life; that he alone will be the one you are aiming to please with your words and your actions. God's Word has so much to teach us about this crucial endeavor that will help us to break the pattern of people pleasing and instead live our lives with confidence. So, let's dive right in and learn together. I am so thankful you have joined us!

Karen

Video: Busting Out of the Prison of People Pleasing (21 MINUTES)

Play the video teaching segment for session one. As you watch, record any thoughts or concepts that stand out to you in the outline that follows.

Notes

The topic of people pleasing is found in Scripture. Perhaps the most relevant verse is Galatians 1:10: "Am I now trying to win the approval of human beings, or of God? Or am I trying to please people? If I were still trying to please people, I would not be a servant of Christ."

One day Karen felt God urging her, "Sweetheart, I'm calling you to have a summer of 'necessary' and 'no.'"

As we view the actions of King Herod, chronicled in Matthew 14, we sense that he had the disease to please.

Herod didn't walk in the fear of the Lord. Instead, he feared the crowds—or on some occasions, certain individuals—which made him act in direct contrast to what he truly believed.

Proverbs 29:25 declares that the fear of humans is a snare. In the Hebrew language, the word translated to *snare* is *moqesh*. This refers to a trapping device for prey, but it also conveys the concept of bait or a lure that entices, reels in, and then drags its victim away.

The Greek word *areskó* in Galatians 1:10 is transliterated to English as *please*. At its core, it means "to agree to satisfy another in order to win their approval, affection, or attention; to meet their expectations; to willingly serve."

There are two different words for *fear* in the Old Testament—*charadah* and *yirah*. *Charadah* means to react with immense anxiety or to tremble with great dread. *Yirah* is defined as responding with extreme awe and thoughtful reverence.

We are all tempted to devour lies when our hearts are unhappy and our souls are hungry.

You do not need their permission to do God's will.

Spotted on a sweatshirt:
"You can't please everyone. You're not pizza."

Group Discussion (30–40 MINUTES)

Take a few minutes to discuss what you just watched in the teaching video session.

1. What part of the video teaching stood out or had the greatest impact on you?

2. When it comes to people pleasing, would you say you generally struggle with it overall in your life or just with a particular person or two? Explain your answer.

3. Has there ever been a time when you, like Karen, felt utterly trapped in the prison of people pleasing with no way out in sight? Briefly share what happened.

4. Take turns having one person from the group look up each of the following verses and passages listed below. In the space after each verse, take a moment to record as many observations as you can about its content after it is read.

  • Galatians 1:10

- Romans 12:1–2

- 1 Thessalonians 2:3–6

- John 12:42–43

- Colossians 3:23–24

- Acts 5:28–29

Are there any guidelines for interacting with others that you can draw out of these verses—both for what to do and what not to do? Take a moment to choose one guideline and list it below, along with which verse you drew the guideline from. Here is one as an example:

> Galatians 1:10: When asked to take on a task or responsibility, before giving the answer, I need to ask myself, "If I say yes, is it because I am trying to win the approval of human beings, or of God?"

Verse: _____

Guideline: _____

_____

_____

_____

5. Take turns having group members share some of the different guidelines for inter-acting with others, along with their corresponding verses.

6. Which of the guidelines just shared do you most need to implement in your life and why?

7. Discuss your thoughts on King Herod that Karen mentioned. Did you learn some-thing new? How did looking at his behavior puzzle, challenge, or motivate you?

8. Karen talked about the Hebrew word for a *snare: moqesh*. This is a trapping device for prey, but it also conveys the concept of bait or a lure that entices, reels in, and then drags its victim away. Have you ever felt trapped by your words or actions because you wanted the approval or admiration of someone else? Briefly tell what happened.

9. Karen mentioned the two different words in the Hebrew language for *fear*. *Charadah* means to react with immense anxiety or trembling with great dread. *Yirah* is defined as to respond with extreme awe and thoughtful reverence. So, we should not react with *charadah* (anxiety and dread) toward others, but we should respond in *yirah* (extreme awe and reverence) toward God. Share with the group your thoughts on these two meanings of the word *fear*. Do you find yourself tempted to *charadah* when it comes to humans? How might you more effectively respond with *yirah* toward God?

10. BONUS QUESTION: Have a few people read 2 Timothy 1:7 aloud to the group in as many Bible translations as you have among you. Then, fill in the following blanks, using the various words you glean from the different Bible versions.

God's Spirit does not _____.
But he does _____.

Now, what is the lesson we glean from 2 Timothy 1:7 when it comes to people pleasing?

11. BONUS QUESTION: In the video, Karen shared this phrase: *"You do not need their permission to do God's will."* Is there a situation in your life where you need to apply this phrase? Share it with the group.

Individual Activity: What Is God Asking Me to Do?

Complete this activity quietly on your own.

Take a moment to get alone in your thoughts, quiet before the Lord. Ask him to reveal one area in your conduct toward a person—or persons—where you need to change. Is there someone you feel controls your behavior because you are afraid to either anger, disappoint, or sadden them? Do you constantly seek the approval of another person or group of people? Is there someone whose opinion you fear more than you fear God? Write down what comes to mind here. (If you personally do not have such a situation, thank God and then spend this time praying for your fellow group members as they do this exercise.)

Now, in your own sweet handwriting, pay attention to the blanks below that are strategically stitched inside Galatians 1:10, BUT don't fill in the missing words. Instead, add the name of someone you identified above.

Am I now trying to win the approval of _____, or of God? Or am I trying to please _____? If I were still trying to please _____, I would not be a servant of Christ.

Session One Memory Verse

Each session has a corresponding—and completely optional—Scripture memory verse or passage. Members may want to come to class five minutes early to practice reciting their verses with others; check to see if anyone is interested in doing this. Then, as a group, read this session's memory verse aloud together:

> "Am I now trying to win the approval of human beings, or of God? Or am I trying to please people? If I were still trying to please people, I would not be a servant of Christ."
> (Galatians 1:10)

Closing Prayer

Have one person close in prayer, focusing on your group's desire to learn to place the healthy and reverent fear of the Lord above the anxiety-producing fear of man. Then, get ready to learn more in your between-sessions personal study before meeting for lesson two!

Between-Sessions Personal Study

Session One Memory Verse

Below is the memory verse for this session. (For your convenience, designed versions of all verses are printed in the back of this study guide beginning on page 135. You may photocopy that page on cardstock or colored paper. Then, cut out the verses and place them in a prominent place—purse, dashboard, desk, kitchen sink—where you can read, study, or memorize. You may want to laminate them if posting them at your kitchen or bathroom sink.) Place each verse where you have easy access to it throughout the day. You may even want to make a digital version as a lock screen for your phone. Set an alarm on your phone for at least two times a day when you know you will have a few minutes to look over the verse and commit it to memory.

"Am I now trying to win the approval of human beings, or of God? Or am I trying to please people? If I were still trying to please people, I would not be a servant of Christ."
(Galatians 1:10)

Read Along and Learn

Read chapters 1–2 of the main book When Making Others Happy Is Making You Miserable. *Use the space below to record any insights you discovered or questions you may want to bring to the next group session.*

What stood out to me in chapter 1:

What I discovered or had thoughts about in chapter 2:

Study and Reflect

1. Flip back through the video teaching notes and the group discussion questions for this session. What most stood out to you? Was it a particular exercise? The Hebrew meaning of one of the words for *fear*? Was it something one of the members of the group said? Write down what it was here.

2. Have you ever known someone who you feel properly feared God rather than people? Jot down a few sentences about this person and how their behavior reflects this principle.

3. In chapter one of *When Making Others Happy Is Making You Miserable*, Karen writes this: "Though our reasons and our personalities may vary, there is one universal result that we see from our constant stream of yeses. It is this: trying to make (or keep) others happy often results in making us miserable" (page 7).

- Have you personally ever felt miserable in the past because you were trying to make someone else happy? If so, describe the situation here:

- After watching the teaching from session one and reading the first two chapters of *When Making Others Happy Is Making You Miserable*, if you could go back in time and handle the situation all over again, what specifically would you do differently?

People pleasing brings such detriment to our lives. We make ourselves miserable. We lie. We create more work for ourselves—both physical and emotional work. We lose grasp of our joy. We offer a standing invitation to regret. This is all so profoundly discouraging. But do you know what is the absolute worst of all?

When we behave this way, we are putting people in the place of God.

When Making Others Happy Is Making You Miserable, page 11

4. The optional memory verse for this session is Galatians 1:10: "Am I now trying to win the approval of human beings, or of God? Or am I trying to please people? If I were still trying to please people, I would not be a servant of Christ." Paul said this in reference to the Judaizers. Members of this group were insisting that converts to Christianity still follow some practices in the Old Testament law, asserting that it was necessary to do so to be a true believer and obtain salvation. Paul corrected this notion, reminding everybody of the true gospel of Christ that offers us salvation by trusting him alone, the One who paved the way to heaven through his death on the cross in our place (Galatians 1:6–7; 3:26).

- Have you ever felt pressure to conform to a spiritual set of guidelines in order to fit in with others? What happened?

- Similarly, have you ever felt pressured to conform to the behavior of others regarding a lifestyle choice, such as your eating plan or how you school your kids?

Finally, using a scale of 1 to 10 (with 1 being "never" and 10 being "always"), use the chart below and on the next page to evaluate areas of your life when it comes to feeling pressured to please an individual or to conform to the behavior of a group of people. These people may be family members, coworkers, friends, or an acquaintance you know from a church or community activity. Write down these people or groups in column one. Record your rating in column two. Finally, jot a phrase or two in the third column about what changes you'd like to make to see that number shift. (You may need additional space if you have more family or work relationships than allowed for in the chart.)

AREA	RATING:	CHANGE I NEED TO MAKE:
Spouse _____		
Child _____		
Child _____		
Child _____		
Child _____		
Child _____		
Extended family member _____		
Extended family member _____		
Extended family member _____		
Extended family member _____		
Coworker _____		
Coworker _____		
Coworker _____		
Friend _____		

AREA	RATING:	CHANGE I NEED TO MAKE:
Friend _____		
Friend _____		
Neighbor _____		
Neighbor _____		
Acquaintance _____		
Acquaintance _____		
Other _____		
Other _____		

- What do you learn from this chart exercise? Are there certain people with whom it is harder for you to resist the urge to people-please? Why do you think this is?

5. In the group session we looked at 2 Timothy 1:7, which reads: "For God has not given us a spirit of fear, but one of power, love, and sound judgment" (CSB).

Now, time to make this verse personal. To do so, fill in the words missing below that sum up the sentiment of the verse.

When I start to feel the pull to people-please, I will remember that God has not given me a _____ of _____. Instead, I can react in _____, showing _____ and exercising _____ _____.

Have your people-pleasing tendencies landed you in a heap of heartache, at least a time or two? Are you tired of outwardly agreeing to something that inwardly you're certain you shouldn't? Does trying to keep everyone happy end up making you quite the opposite? Are you in desperate need of your own season of necessary and no? And—if you're completely honest—would you admit that sometimes you put people in the place of God?

When Making Others Happy Is Making You Miserable, page 16

6. Proverbs 29:25 states: "Fear of man will prove to be a snare, but whoever trusts in the Lord is kept safe."

In chapter two of *When Making Others Happy Is Making You Miserable*, Karen writes about the Hebrew word for *snare*, which is *moqesh*. She says,

Is there a relationship in your life where your heartstrings are constantly tugged? You never want to upset this person because so much of their life is filled with sadness and you aren't interested in adding more disappointment. And perhaps, worst of all, is there someone with whom you have a dysfunctional relationship, and you dread ever making them upset, so you constantly take the bait and give in, just to please them?

If you answered yes to any of the above questions—or can think of another scenario where you are tempted to please someone constantly—you, my friend, have been caught in a *moqesh*.

- How does the image of a trap or snare accurately apply to situations where you are tempted to please someone or gain their attention or approval?

7. We can become free from the trap of pleasing humans when we place the proper reverent fear of the Lord above the improper, anxiety-inducing fear of man. A quick online search for fear of the Lord will unearth at least twenty-five verses, depending on which translation of the Bible you use. Below are just a few references to the fear of the Lord—what it is, and what it does for us. Look up each of the verses either in your Bible or on an online site such as biblegateway.com. After each one, jot any key words that stand out to you from reading the verse. Pay special attention to any vivid verbs or adjectives that pertain to what the definition of "the fear of the Lord" is or to what action you are to take. Then, read Karen's additional thoughts on each verse to ponder.

> **VERSE:** Proverbs 9:1
> **KEY WORDS:** _____
> **TO PONDER:** In many instances, the fear of the Lord is directly tethered to the idea of wisdom and knowledge. The Hebrew word for *wisdom* in the Old Testament often referred to skill in one's work or in military battle, shrewdness in dealing with people, or prudence in dealing with religious affairs.
>
> **VERSE:** Proverbs 1:7
> **KEY WORDS:** _____
> **TO PONDER:** This verse asserts that the fear of the Lord is the "beginning" of knowledge. What exactly is meant by beginning? The Hebrew definition isn't only referencing the starting point, though a starting place is certainly implied. The word *beginning* here also means "the choicest, finest, foremost," as in the first fruits of a harvest.

VERSE: Psalm 112:1

KEY WORDS: _____

TO PONDER: When we fear God, Scripture calls us blessed. In some Bible translations it reads *happy* or *joyful*. (And hey, who doesn't want to be blessed, happy, or joyful?) The Old Testament Hebrew term first used here is *esher. This word* simply means "how very happy!" Fearing God, rather than trying relentlessly to make humans happy, will, in the end, bring delight to us if we follow his commands over the desires of others.

VERSE: Proverbs 14:2

KEY WORDS: _____

TO PONDER: To walk uprightly in this verse means "correctly, honestly, and with utmost integrity." Contrast that with people pleasing, which at times is thinly glazed with untruths as we say what we sense the other person wants to hear. When we do, our integrity might be harmed.

VERSE: Psalm 34:11

KEY WORDS: _____

TO PONDER: Did you catch it? The fear of the Lord must be learned. We may not come by it naturally, but we can be taught to do it. With a little intention, we can acquire the ability to fear the Lord.

It is the fear of humans that produces anxiety in our minds, dread in our hearts, and even trembling in our bodies. Unhealthy apprehension causes us to be at the mercy of the person of whom we are frightened. But having a proper reverence and fear of God will not cause us such emotional and physical distress. It will lead us to a place of quiet confidence—even happiness—when we learn to obey his commands, even at those times when it might upset others.

When Making Others Happy Is Making You Miserable, page 32

8. In chapter two of *When Making Others Happy Is Making You Miserable*, Karen writes:

> Will you dare to become the "Decider in Chief" of your own life, making choices based on what God wants you to do rather than on what people want you to? We must own our lives. Our lives are made up of our actions. Our actions result from our thoughts. Our thoughts are formed when we respond to others' behavior. And our responses must be in line with God's Word, carried out with confidence not timidity.
>
> Perhaps it's time we stopped assigning the wrong value to others, giving them power over our emotions. Of course, we are going to need to spend the rest of our lives interacting with others and navigating relationships. But we need not fear the slinging of opinions that may happen or the reactions of others when they view our choices. Oh, how I wish I could go back to my former self, at so many junctions in life, and preach this sermon to her!

- She then lists sermons she wishes she could preach to her old self at various stages in her life (pages 37–38.) If you could go back in time, what sermons would you preach to your former self? Write at least one or two of them in the space provided below.

Scripture Memory Verse Reminder

Here again is our verse for this week. Practice saying it again to solidify it deep in your mind.

"Am I now trying to win the approval of human beings, or of God? Or am I trying to please people? If I were still trying to please people, I would not be a servant of Christ." (Galatians 1:10)

Just Who Is Calling the Shots?

Session Two Memory Verse

"On the contrary, we speak as those approved by God to be entrusted with the gospel. We are not trying to please people but God, who tests our hearts." (1 Thessalonians 2:4)

Welcome to session two of *When Making Others Happy Is Making You Miserable.* In our time together we will encounter the various types of people who often try to control our behavior, whether overtly or ever-so-subtly. Most importantly, we'll discover how to ensure that we are following God rather than being manipulated or influenced by others. Let's jump right in and determine to allow God to call the shots in our lives rather than delegating that task to people.

Karen

In-Between Sessions Review (10 MINUTES)

Spend 10 minutes allowing group members to share what each got out of the in-between sessions work since the last time you met. Was there something that challenged you? Did you learn something new? Did you feel convicted by something or had questions for the other group members? Spend time discussing what the group members discovered before watching the session two video.

Video: Just Who is Calling the Shots? (23 MINUTES)

Play the video teaching segment for session two. As you watch, record any thoughts or concepts that stand out to you in the notes section that follows.

Notes

Sometimes our personality types set us up for granting the wishes of others regardless of what it does to us.

There are many sorts of people pleasers. Often, they are achievers who view being liked as the ultimate achievement. However, they may also be givers, perfectionists, peace-makers, rescuers, helpers, lovers, and behind-the-scenes do-ers.

Any personality strength carried to an extreme can soon become a lingering liability.

It isn't just our own personality that comes into play. There are also varied personality types in our lives who want to get us to do what they desire.

The types of people who often try to control our thinking and behavior often fall into four categories:

- Pushers

- Pouters

- Guilt-Bombers

- Me-First Maximizers

The New Testament character Pontius Pilate seemed to be doing everything he could think of to release Jesus. However, rather than do what he knew was right, he instead bowed to the will of the crowd (Luke 23:1–25; John 19:1–16; Matthew 27:11–26; Mark 15:1–15).

Not everyone around Pilate pressured him to hand Jesus over for crucifixion. His wife stood alone as the voice of reason, telling him he should have nothing to do with killing Jesus (Matthew 27:19).

There are times we should make choices in accordance with what someone else is suggesting. The time to do this is when their advice lines up with, or does not violate, God's Word.

When we allow others to call the shots, we are putting people in the place of God.

In trying to please all, he had pleased none.

—Aesop, *Aesop's Fables*

Group Discussion (25–35 MINUTES)

Take a few minutes to discuss what you just watched in the teaching video session.

1. In the video, Karen talked about personality tests. Have you ever taken one and what—if anything—do you remember about the results? Did they surprise you or did they confirm what you already suspected about your personality makeup?

2. Karen mentioned that sometimes due to our personality type, we have a hard time preventing ourselves from falling into the people-pleasing trap. She specifically mentioned these types of people: achievers, givers, perfectionists, peacemakers, rescuers, helpers, lovers, and behind-the-scenes do-ers. Do you identify with any of these personality types? Tell the group which one best describes you and what part this plays in giving in to the desires of others.

3. Here is a quote from the video teaching: "Any personality strength carried to an extreme can soon become a lingering liability." Have you seen this play out in your own life and, if so, how?

4. What are your thoughts about the types of people—the Pushers, Pouters, Guilt-Bombers, and Me-First Maximizers—who often try to control our thinking and behavior? Which of these four categories do you think is hardest for you to deal with, and why do you think this is so? (Do not mention any specific people or situations in particular; just talk about the category of people as a whole.)

5. Now more specifically, as a group, go back through the four categories of people, giving members the opportunity to mention a specific example of how they were affected by someone with this type of behavior. (NOTE: To prevent this from crossing the line into gossip, be sure members do not give names or identify the people they are citing in any way. Just focus on the behavior, your feelings about it, and what your response to it was.)

- A Pusher

- A Pouter

- A Guilt-Bomber

- A Me-First Maximizer

6. In the video teaching, we explored the behavior of the New Testament official Pontius Pilate who was a Roman governor in the region of Judea where Jesus lived. He seemed to try to think of a way to release Jesus. However, rather than do what he knew was right, he instead bowed to the will of the crowd.

Have someone read John 18:28–19:16 aloud to the group and then answer the questions below.

- What verses seem to hint that Pontius Pilate was trying to find a reason to release Jesus from custody? What words or phrases make you think this?

- What words or phrases in this passage are indications of the emotions Pilate was experiencing? State any verses where you find your answer.

- At one point Pilate seems to give a very flippant response to Jesus by tossing out a question to him. What question did he ask and in what verse do you find it? Instead, can we use this question he raised in a positive manner when deciding if we will give in to the desires, expectations, or requests of the people in our lives?

- Ultimately, Pilate rejected the truth of who Jesus was and gave in to the will of the people. He had Jesus flogged and later sent away for crucifixion. The pressure of people made him do something that was totally against what he really believed. Can you think of a time in your life when pressure from an individual, or even a group of people, made you do something you really didn't want to do? Briefly share this experience with the group.

7. Think back to any example that you gave earlier of a Pusher, Pouter, Guilt-Bomber, or Me-First Maximizer in your life. If you could go back in time and handle the situation differently, what adjustments to your behavior would you make? Is there a specific verse, word, or phrase from the last question that prompts you to want to alter your behavior?

8. Let's talk progress going forward. Now that you've had some time to both view the teaching and discuss this topic as a group, think of a sentence or two to speak to yourself that could help you deal with each of these categories of people in the future. Here is one example:

   For the Guilt-Bomber: I will not confuse false guilt from another person who is trying to trap me into doing things their way with true conviction from God about wrong or sinful behavior.

First, take a few moments of silence to write out any sentences you can think of. Then have group members share any thoughts that they wish with the entire group.

- Pushers

- Pouters

- Guilt-Bombers

- Me-First Maximizers

9. BONUS QUESTION: On page 44 of *When Making Others Happy Is Making You Miserable* is this quote from author Edward Welch. It explains his concept of how we give people in our lives various "shapes." He writes,

> Notice some of the common shapes we give others:
> People are gas pumps that fill us.
> People are sought-after tickets to acceptance and fame.
> People are priests who have the power to make us feel clean and okay.
> People are terrorists. We never know when they will strike next.
> People are dictators whose every word is law. They are in complete control.*

---

* Edward Welch, *When People are Big and God is Small* (Phillipsburg, NJ: P & R Publishing, 1997), 181.

Which of the word pictures he gives in this quote most catches your attention and why? Can you think of a specific example of when that particular "shape" showed up in your life?

10. BONUS QUESTION: Perhaps you have heard it said before that there is a God-shaped hole in each human heart that only Jesus can fill. What would you say is important for us to remember when it comes to allowing God to fill the holes in our hearts rather than let others in our lives take on that critical role?

Individual Activity: What Is God Asking Me to Do? (5 MINUTES)

Complete this activity on your own.

Take a moment to get alone in your thoughts, sitting quiet before the Lord. Be honest about the ways in which you have allowed certain people and personalities to dictate your behavior or shape your thoughts rather than allowing God to be the One to do so. Then, in the space provided below, write a one- or two-sentence declaration about how he would like this to be different going forward.

Session Two Memory Verse

As a group, read this session's memory verse aloud together:

> "On the contrary, we speak as those approved by God to be entrusted with the gospel.
> We are not trying to please people but God, who tests our hearts." (1 Thessalonians 2:4)

Closing Prayer

Have one person close in prayer, focusing on your group's desire to stop letting others push you, guilt you, manipulate you, or take the place of God in your life. Ask him to give you the courage and strength to place his opinion above all others. Then, get ready to learn more in your between-sessions personal study before meeting for session three!

Between-Sessions Personal Study

"On the contrary, we speak as those approved by God to be entrusted with the gospel. We are not trying to please people but God, who tests our hearts." (1 Thessalonians 2:4)

Read Along and Learn

Read chapter 3 of the book When Making Others Happy Is Making You Miserable. *Use the space below to record any insights you discovered or questions you may want to bring to the next group session.*

What most stood out to me in this chapter:

Study and Reflect

1. Review your notes from the teaching for session two. What most stood out to you and why? Was it something that challenged you? Was it a concept you have been struggling with for a while? Was it some "aha moment" that you think will help you in your future dealings with people who try to pressure you? Write it in the space below.

2. On the continuum below, place an X near the spot that best describes you and your interactions with those people you know who habitually try to call the shots in your life.

   When it comes to people who pressure me to think or behave a certain way, my customary pattern has been to give in to their wishes:

   Never   Rarely   Once in a while   Somewhat frequently   Almost always

   I would say this is most usually due to: (circle one)

   My personality   The personalities of others   A combination of both

   Which of the four types of controllers do you most struggle with? Circle it and then, in the space following it, explain why in a sentence or two.

   • Pushers

   • Pouters

- Guilt-Bombers

- Me-First Maximizers

3. In Colossians 3:23, the apostle Paul urges the church family in Colossae with this directive: "Whatever you do, work at it with all your heart, as working for the Lord, not for human masters . . ." The Greek word for *work* is *ergazomai*. It means "to do, work, acquire by trade, or to practice." However, it also means "to perform." If we think about this verse in relation to allowing others to control our behavior, how are we in fact working—or performing—for them instead of for God?

How is working (or performing) for others instead of seeking to determine what God would have us do a direct violation of the instructions in this verse?

4. In Galatians 5:16, Paul states, "So I say, walk by the Spirit, and you will not gratify the desires of the flesh." Sometimes our flesh simply wants to be liked. It feels good. It wins us friends and can make us popular. And so, we give in and either talk, or behave, in a manner we know will please someone in our life. How can the truth of this verse empower us to stop such behavior? What do you think is the correlation between walking in the Spirit and not caving in to people pleasing?

Yes, many of us people-please due to our personality makeup. However, sometimes the "disease to please" rears its annoying head because we get to a place where we allow others to fill a role in our lives they were never meant to occupy.

When Making Others Happy Is Making You Miserable, page 44

5. It's not always wrong to want to please others. In fact, there are many times that we should. The truth is, there is a fine line between obeying what God says in his Word about how we are to treat others and outright people-pleasing. Look up the following verses and then below them, write your thoughts about who we are to seek to please as well as why and how we are to do this.

- **VERSES:** Ephesians 6:1–3; Colossians 3:20
- **WHO:**

  _____

- **WHY** and **HOW:**

  _____

  _____

- **VERSES:** Ephesians 6:5–8
- **WHO:**

  _____

- **WHY** and **HOW:**

  _____

  _____

- **VERSES:** Ephesians 5:15–33
- **WHO:**

  _____

- **WHY** and **HOW:**

  _____

  _____

- **VERSES:** Romans 13:1–7
- **WHO:**

  _____

- **WHY** and **HOW:**

  _____

  _____

- **VERSE:** Romans 15:2
- **WHO:**

  _____

- **WHY** and **HOW:**

  _____

  _____

After reading these verses, what questions can we ask ourselves when it comes to pleasing others that will help determine whether we are doing it because God commands us to or because we feel pressured to do so or doing it to be liked?

God's Word makes some very true observations about the company we keep and also offers us wise counsel in this area. Proverbs 13:20 instructs us to, "Walk with the wise and become wise . . ." Why? Here is the rest of the verse: ". . . for a companion of fools suffers harm." Additionally, 1 Corinthians 15:33 warns, "Do not be misled: 'Bad company corrupts good character.'"

If you are navigating some difficulties with people in your life who pressure you to make certain decisions or even dive in and manipulate or control you, have you ever thought it may be time to put some distance between you and them? Take a few moments to pray about whether there is anyone with whom you are now closely associated who might be corrupting your character and causing you harm. Then, for your eyes only, drop that person's name down in the space below.

What are some actions you might take, beginning now, that will help you stop capitulating to that person and take your marching orders from God instead? Do be cautious though. The reason to place some distance between you and the other person is not necessarily to sever the relationship but to help it improve in the future. Write down any action steps you will take below.

6. Because we may have formed a habit over the years of allowing others to dictate what we say or do, it becomes very hard to break the pattern. We might know that we should behave differently, but we are so tempted to just keep giving in, acquiescing repeatedly so we don't cause any relational waves. But God is more than able to help us in our temptation to give in.

First Corinthians 10:13 states, "No temptation has come upon you except what is common to humanity. But God is faithful; he will not allow you to be tempted beyond what you are able, but with the temptation he will also provide the way out so that you may be able to bear it" (CSB).

Stop and read that verse again, very slowly. Then, fill in the blanks in the paragraph below that will help you to boldly state your intentions going forward and remind you to choose God over caving in to people.

When I am tempted in the future to cave-in to the desires of others, I will remember that _____ temptation I am experiencing is unique. In fact, it is _____ to humanity. But, God is _____. He will not allow me to be tempted _____ what I am _____. Instead, with the temptation he will also provide the _____ _____ so that I will be able to _____ _____.

Now, in your own words, craft a one- or two-sentence prayer requesting God's help in your temptation rather than letting others influence your behavior.

Are you ready to deal with the shot-callers in your life, the ones who get you to do what they want you to do without you ever even putting up a fuss? It will sting for a minute as you rip that capitulating behavior out of your repertoire of responses. However, being controlled by others and their pushy, pouty, guilt-giving, or self-serving way is not honoring to God. You are living your life according to their will, not his. My friends, this is not a healthy way to live.

When Making Others Happy Is Making You Miserable, page 55

7. This session's key memory verse is 1 Thessalonians 2:4, which reads,

> "On the contrary, we speak as those approved by God to be entrusted with the gospel. We are not trying to please people but God, who tests our hearts."

Read over the verse and then use it to fill in the blanks below.

How do we speak? We speak as those _____ by _____. With what are we believers entrusted? We are entrusted with the _____. We are not trying to please _____ but to please _____ who _____ our _____.

The gospel is the most crucial message in the history of humanity. And we, as followers of Christ, have been entrusted with this important message. What exactly does *entrusted* mean?

The Greek word for *entrusted* is *pisteuó*. It is derived from the root word *pistis* which means faith or belief. *Pisteuó* differs ever so slightly in that it conveys the concept of passing something to someone and trusting them completely with it. God has trusted us with the gospel message. Of course, we should use our words to tell others about the gospel—the Good News of Jesus—and how Christ's death, burial, and resurrection offers us a place in heaven if we respond and place our trust in him. Additionally—though not a part of salvation but rather our response to being saved—we should seek to follow God's commands and live according to the directives we find in Scripture.

So, how is letting other people, rather than God, dictate how you live contrary to the gospel message that we have been entrusted to show the world?

What is one action step you hope to take that will help you stop placing people in the place of God but rather seek to obey him instead of humans? Write it below. You may even want to write it on a sticky note to place where you will see it often.

Scripture Memory Verse Reminder

Here again is our focus verse for this week. Take a moment to read it aloud and try to commit it to memory.

"On the contrary, we speak as those approved by God to be entrusted with the gospel. We are not trying to please people but God, who tests our hearts." (1 Thessalonians 2:4)

Session Three

To Tell the Truth

Welcome to session three of *When Making Others Happy Is Making You Miserable.* During our study together we will confront a hard reality. Although there may be many reasons why we fall into the pattern of people pleasing, we have to admit that when we do it, often we are being dishonest. We say and do things we really don't mean just to please someone else. Let's jump right in and tackle this difficult truth as we continue our time together.

Karen

In-Between Sessions Review (10 MINUTES)

Spend 10 minutes allowing group members to share what each got out of the in-between sessions work since the last time you met. Was there something that challenged you? Did you learn something new? Did you feel challenged by something or have questions for the other group members? Spend time discussing that before watching the session three video.

Video: To Tell the Truth (19 MINUTES)

Play the video teaching segment for session three. As you watch, record any thoughts or concepts that stand out to you in the outline that follows.

Notes

One Sunday morning Karen sat in church and heard a stark—but true—statement made by her pastor: *People pleasers often lie.*

Deception in the life of a people pleaser gets cleverly cloaked as concern and care.

God told Abraham, first called Abram, that he would be the father of many nations (Genesis 15:5; 22:17). His wife Sarah, known as Sarai at the time, was childless. When God's promise about being an heir didn't take place in the timeline Abraham had hoped for, he took matters into his own hands.

A half-truth is still a whole lie.

The Hebrew concept of a double heart means someone who really has two hearts—one that is true to their inner soul and one that is portrayed to the person hearing their dishonesty.

As followers of Christ, we are called to speak the truth in love (Ephesians 4:15).

The Greek word for *truth* in Ephesians 4:15 is *alétheuó*. It means speaking Spirit-led, honest words that match God's truth so others can live in reality instead of in personal illusion.

Sometimes being truthful brings tension. The only other instance of the word *alétheuó* in Scripture is in Galatians 4:16 where Paul states that some friends did not like it when he spoke the truth to them.

Let's stop putting others in the place of God, elevating their opinions about us above him and his view.

Honesty saves everyone's time.
—Anonymous

Group Discussion (25–35 MINUTES)

Take a few minutes to discuss what you just watched in the teaching video session.

1. Can you think of a time in childhood when you told a lie but were later found out? Briefly share what happened.

2. What were your initial thoughts when you heard Karen make this statement: *"People pleasers often lie"*? Do you agree? Disagree? Did it make you feel uneasy or cause any interactions with others to pop into your mind?

    What jumped out most to you in the video teaching about the story of Abraham and Sarah?

3. Have you yourself ever told a half-truth? Would you be willing to share that situation with the group?

    How could reminding yourself of the statement "a half-truth is still a whole lie" prevent you from shading the truth in the future?

4. Have someone in the group read Ephesians 4:20–25 and Colossians 3:9–10 aloud in a few different translations. (If members don't have differing translations in their Bibles, hop on biblegateway.com to view more.) Then answer the questions below.

Why do you think the apostle Paul uses the word picture of putting off old things and putting on new ones? What does this indicate about our behavior before we became believers contrasted with our behavior now that we follow Christ?

Think of the concept of putting off and putting on with regards to clothing. How often do we put off or put on clothing? What does this suggest about putting off your old self and putting on your new self—especially when it comes to lying and speaking the truth? Is it something we do once at the point of salvation or is it something we continually do? And if you think it is the latter, what are some practical ways you have found to do this?

The tail end of Ephesians 4:25 reads like this in various translations:

- "... for we are all members of one body." (NIV)
- "... because we are members of one another." (CSB)
- "... and we are all parts of the body of Christ." (AMP)

Why do you think Paul stresses that telling the truth is important for us as members of one body—the body of Jesus Christ? How have you seen lying hurt the church body in the past?

5. Psalm 34 was written by David when he pretended to be insane before King Abimelech. At the time, David was attempting to escape from Saul's pursuit, so he fled to the Philistine city of Gath but found no refuge there. Afterward, David journeyed to the cave at Adullam where other distressed men joined him. This surprisingly joy-filled psalm appears to have been written as David hid in that cave. The backstory can help us to remember that joy can still come out of even our deepest, darkest times in life.

This psalm is an acrostic, meaning each new verse begins with another letter of the Hebrew alphabet (with the exception of the Hebrew letter *waw*). Such psalms were written in this pattern to help people more easily memorize them.

Let's survey Psalm 34:12–15 together, written here in the NIV version. Have one group member read the passage aloud. Then, answer the questions that follow.

> [12] Whoever of you loves life
>   and desires to see many good days,
> [13] keep your tongue from evil
>   and your lips from telling lies.
> [14] Turn from evil and do good;
>   seek peace and pursue it.
> [15] The eyes of the LORD are on the righteous,
>   and his ears are attentive to their cry;

Review the nonnegotiables in this passage—the directives from God; the commands we are to follow if we want to "see many good days."

Which of these nonnegotiables would you say is something you currently need to pursue in your life? Is it keeping your lips from telling lies? Is it seeking or pursuing peace? If you care to share with the group the reason why you selected that particular nonnegotiable, do so.

In addition to the directives from this passage that we are supposed to carry out, we also see a promise from the Lord. What is that promise and in which verse did you spot it?

How is this promise a comfort to us as we seek to be someone who tells the truth to others, rather than someone who caves into lying to please or appease others?

6. Some relational experts suggest, when telling a hard truth to someone, you use what is called the "sandwich method." This tool is a method of delivery that wraps negative content in a pocket of praise. The discussion starts with positive comments and is followed by the hard truth. However, before ending the exchange, positive words are used again. This helps to soften the sharp edges of the truth and makes the hearer more receptive to receiving the news. Think of the hard-to-hear words being the meat and the cheese that are packed between words of praise, which are the slices of bread.

Rotate having members of the group read aloud each of the following verses from the book of Proverbs, allowing time for recording any key words or concepts. After all the verses have been read, explain how the words and phrases you recorded can assist you in speaking to someone using the sandwich method—mixing hard truth with gentleness and kindness.

Proverbs 11:9

Proverbs 12:17

Proverbs 12:25

Proverbs 15:1

Proverbs 15:4

Proverbs 16:24

Can you think of a time in your life when you were not completely honest, but instead chose to lie to someone because you either feared their reaction or feared hurting their feelings? Briefly tell the group about the situation. Also tell how you might have used the wisdom in these verses, in the form of the sandwich method, to speak truthfully—but also respectfully and kindly—to that person.

7. Time to do a little crowdsourcing. Let's brainstorm together some ways to gently introduce some truth telling into our conversations. Below is a situation you might happen across in life where you might be tempted to shade the truth rather than be forthright. Do a little creative quick thinking to come up with a well-worded introduction that might help you speak the truth in love in the given situation. But first, two examples have been done for you to help you understand the process.

> **SITUATION ONE:** Your close friend asked you your opinion on the sweater she just put on. The truth is that it is a tad tight on her, causing the buttons on the front of it to pull. Also, the color is rather dark and drab and does not blend well with her pale skin tone but rather makes her look older than she is. You want to be truthful, but not hurt her feelings.

> **QUICK THINKING:** You decide you will not lie and say the garment looks good on her. You also recall a sweater she wore a few weeks ago that was pale aqua and really accentuated her light blue eyes. You decide you are going to attempt to tell the truth gently by offering an alternative solution.

> **GENTLE INTRO:** Well, even though I really like the material and the style of that sweater, I think the one you wore a few weeks ago that was pale aqua looked better on you. The shape of it was very flattering and it really made your blue eyes pop. Maybe you should wear that one instead?

> ———

> **SITUATION TWO:** A coworker of yours is very excited because she and her husband decided they want to buy a brand-new car. You know they struggle financially but were lured in by a salesperson with the promise of a long loan with a low interest rate. You not only feel that this hefty new monthly payment will strap her financially, but you also know that the value of a brand-new car decreases as soon as you drive it off the lot. You don't want to squelch their excitement, but you want to speak some level-headed truth into the situation.

> **QUICK THINKING:** You remember a recent article you read online by a financial expert who told why it is not good for someone on a tight budget to buy a

brand-new car. You also think of a friend who recently got a car from a leasing company that was only three years old and had hardly been used.

GENTLE INTRO: How exciting for you that you're getting a new vehicle! I am so thrilled for you. I don't want to squelch your excitement, but I do feel as your friend that I want to share a little information with you that might help you in your decision and potentially save you some money. Experts say that the value of a brand-new car diminishes as soon as you drive it off the lot. However, there are some really great places where you can get cars that are only two or three years old and have been used by a leasing company with very little miles, mostly highway miles. Would you like me to send you the links to some of those places? Maybe you could find a great vehicle you love for thousands of dollars less.

Okay, it's your turn. Work on these as individuals and then go through the situation as a group, allowing members to read their answers out loud.

SITUATION: Your close friend wants to try out for the community's vocal ensemble that will perform at the town festival this summer. However, they really have no singing talent. In fact, the old saying that they "can't carry a tune in a bucket" could certainly apply. You are certain they will not be selected because there are over fifty people auditioning for only twelve spots. However, they may be a perfect fit for other potential roles in the town's festival. They are highly organized and great at brainstorming ideas, and the festival committee is looking for more steering team members. No matter what you say, they may still audition, and it is quite possible that God wants to teach them to be a graceful loser. However, as their friend, you feel some honesty will help them make the best decision.

Now, complete the rest of this exercise below.

QUICK THINKING:

_____

_____

_____

GENTLE INTRO:

_____

_____

_____

8. Have a few group members read Proverbs 15:1 aloud, each using a different translation. Explore at least three or four different ones. Then, as a group, complete the following exercise in your study guide. Be sure to check out the CEB (Common English Bible) version on a site such as biblegateway.com.

What kind of answer are we encouraged to give? Write down all the different adjectives that describe such an answer that you found in the various translations you read. You may wish to have them read out loud again.

In Hebrew, the word translated to our English as _soft, gentle,_ or _sensitive,_ is _rak._ This word in its original language translates to our English words _tender, soft, refined,_ or _delicate._ Now let's look further at this verse.

What does this particular type of answer do? Jot down all the different words that describe the result of giving a soft answer that you discover in the various versions of this verse. Again, explore various translations, making sure to hop online and check out the NLT (New Living Translation) and CEV (Contemporary English Version) translations.

Now, let's dissect the rest of this important Scripture. What kind of response are we cautioned _not_ to give? Record the phrases you read in the various translations.

In the original Hebrew, this word means "hurtful," "painful," "grievous," or "sorrowful," and it is often used with regard to wounding or hurting someone's mind.

Finally, what does this sort of harsh response do? Write down the various phrases you glean from the translations that are read by group members. Be sure to check out the NLT translation.

The phrase "stirs up anger" or "makes tempers flare" in the Hebrew language paints a picture of climbing upward or of escalating human anger.

CHALLENGE: Time to "say it in a sentence." Take just a moment to look back over what you wrote down as you looked closely at the concepts in this verse. How would you restate this verse using your own words? Have group members who would like to share their answer do so.

Finally, how could this verse help you in the future when you are trying to speak truthfully and not people-please but likewise desire be sensitive to the heart and mind of the one to whom you are speaking?

9. BONUS QUESTION: Celebration time! We are at the halfway point of the study! Knowing what you have learned so far about what the Bible says about pleasing God rather than others, how might you conduct yourself differently in a relationship where you feel the constant compulsion to please? Share with the group what you hope will change.

Individual Activity: What Is God Asking Me to Do?

Complete this activity on your own.

Take a moment to talk to the Lord silently. Ask him to reveal to you whether dishonesty—even in an attempt to prevent hurting someone's feelings—is an issue in your life. Ask him to bring to your mind any recent instances where you lied or any people with whom you continually have trouble being honest. Then, write out a one- to three-sentence prayer asking the Lord for help in this area.

Session Three Memory Verse

As a group, read this session's memory verse out loud together:

"And stop lying to each other. You have given up your old way of life with its habits." (Colossians 3:9 CEV)

Closing Prayer

Have one person close in prayer, focusing on your group's desire to be honest and yet kind and compassionate. Then, get ready to learn more in your between-sessions personal study before meeting for session four!

Session Three

Between-Sessions
Personal Study

Session Three Memory Verse

"And stop lying to each other. You have given up your old way of life with its habits."
(Colossians 3:9 CEV)

Read Along and Learn

Read chapter 4 of When Making Others Happy Is Making You Miserable. *Use the space below to record any insights you discovered or questions you may want to bring to the next group session.*

What stood out to me in chapter 4:

Study and Reflect

1. Review what you wrote down in your study guide during your group time together for this session. What is one biblical truth that stood out to you? Was it a particular verse you had read before, or one that spoke to you in a new way? What scriptural concept is your favorite of the session?

2. Pore over the following phrases, one row at a time. Circle the one that is most closely descriptive of you. Then, answer the questions below the chart.

A	B
I often shade the truth to prevent hurt feelings.	I tell the truth even though I know it might sting.
I'm anxious when I want to give an opinion that differs from the majority of people present.	I'm never afraid to give my opinion.
When speaking a hard truth, my greatest concern is doing it carefully and kindly.	I just tell the truth regardless of who's hearing it.
I don't like to voice my displeasure to someone.	Expressing displeasure rarely bothers me.
I worry that my honesty might cost me a friendship.	I think friends should be able to handle the truth.

Are most of your answers in the A column or B column?

Okay. Keep you result of that little exercise tucked in your mind and read on.

Isn't it astonishing how Scripture speaks to people with various personalities and approaches to life? Let's look at one example found in Ephesians 4:15. Here is that verse written out for you in the CSB (Christian Standard Bible) translation:

"But speaking the truth in love, let us grow in every way into him who is the head—Christ."

When it comes to both speaking the truth and doing it in a loving manner, what often happens in our behavior is that we tend to gravitate toward one of two opposite concepts in this verse, depending on our personalities. Some of us find it easier to straight-up speak the truth, but we don't always do it in the most loving manner. (This type of person probably picked mostly column B for their answers.) Others of us surmise that the only loving thing is to not tell the truth at all. (This would apply to people who selected column A most of the time.)

Do you find yourself leaning more toward one way than the other? Write a few sentences here declaring how you want to more accurately perform both actions found in this verse—speak in a truthful manner but also speak with a loving approach.

3. We are going to spend some time in this session looking at the New Testament character of Peter. Peter was one of the twelve disciples of Jesus, included among Christ's inner circle. However, as the time grew close for Jesus to be handed over for crucifixion, Peter began to have a little problem with lying. Read the following passages to familiarize yourself with this situation. Then answer the questions that follow.

    Matthew 26:31–35
    Matthew 26:57–75
    Luke 22:54–62

Look back over the passages. In which verses does Peter declare his bold allegiance to Jesus and his promise to never betray him?

In which verses do we find Peter not speaking truthfully about knowing Jesus or being closely associated with him?

If you were a lawyer arguing on Peter's behalf, give your best case for why he decided to lie. What might telling the truth have done to him?

Do your words sometimes just tumble off your tongue without you giving vigilant thought to what you're saying? Especially when we are trying to defuse conflict before it even starts, we sometimes panic. We say things we really don't mean all in an effort to keep things at an even keel. What if instead, we prayerfully, thoughtfully, and carefully chose our words, being totally truthful but in a way that shows our sincerity and does not lead to conflict.

When Making Others Happy Is Making You Miserable, page 70

4. Now let's explore another passage that mentions Peter. However, you will notice in this chunk of Scripture a brand new and improved Peter, not one who is quaking in his boots and cowering in a corner and then lying when asked a question that might make his life uncomfortable—or even worse—if he told the truth. Instead, he is bold. Forthright. A completely changed human. Read Acts 4:1–22 and then answer the questions that follow.

In the beginning of Acts 4, what resulted in the life of the people who heard Peter speaking? Cite the verse or verses where you find your answer.

When the rulers, elders, and teachers of the law met in Jerusalem, soon Peter and his companion John were brought before them and questioned. They were told to reveal what was giving them power or in whose name they were acting when they'd recently healed a lame man. From verse 8, what do you notice that is significant about what happened to Peter before he began to speak?

How might this help you pray more specifically about the times when you want to speak truthfully but are afraid the results might not be so wonderful for you? Whose help should you elicit before opening your mouth?

The once scared and scattered Peter transforms before our eyes in this chapter. What did people notice about Peter and John in Acts 4:13?

Peter and John were seized and put in jail (Acts 4:3). Later, they were commanded not to speak or teach at all in the name of Jesus (Acts 4:18). But neither of these things stopped them even though it might cause them great distress, imprisonment, or maybe even death. How did they respond? Give the verses where you find your answer.

The authorities threaten Peter and John further, but ultimately let them go. Why? Give the verse where you locate this reason.

Taking into account all the passages you read about Peter, what was the key that empowered him to speak the truth boldly?

Now, turn this information into a prayer. Write a few sentences here as a prayer to God, asking him to empower you with the Holy Spirit and enable you to speak up, speak out, and tell the truth, even when the results might not be pleasant.

5. Psalm 15 was written by David and it describes the character of a person who is welcomed into the presence of the Lord. Read the psalm at a normal reading pace. Then, reread it and complete the exercises that follow.

Psalm 15
A psalm of David.

1 LORD, who may dwell in your sacred tent?
    Who may live on your holy mountain?
2 The one whose walk is blameless,
    who does what is righteous,
    who speaks the truth from their heart;
3 whose tongue utters no slander,
    who does no wrong to a neighbor,
    and casts no slur on others;
4 who despises a vile person
    but honors those who fear the LORD;

who keeps an oath even when it hurts,
    and does not change their mind;
⁵ who lends money to the poor without interest;
    who does not accept a bribe against the innocent.
Whoever does these things
    will never be shaken.

Grab a colorful pen, highlighter, or colored pencil and scan this psalm for any words or phrases that tell an action to be taken or a characteristic to possess. For example, in verse 2, you would choose "whose walk is blameless" or in verse 4 you would select "who keeps an oath even when it hurts." Highlight or circle as many as you can find.

Are you back? Good. Now, to the right of any of the lines that you highlighted or circled, write a few words of direction to yourself about how to behave based on the phrases in this psalm. Example, to the right of the first line of verse 2, you would write, "Walk blamelessly." In verse 4 you might write, "Even though it is painful, keep your word."

Now, carefully look over what you wrote. Pray that God will show you just one or two of these directives that you need to focus on in your life. Put a star beside any that you choose.

Finally, write a one-sentence prayer to God below about the directions or commands you chose. Then finish it up by copying the last line of the psalm: *"Whoever does these things will never be shaken."*

People pleasers are also deceivers. We do not always speak the truth. We shade it. Skirt it. Dress it up just a tad before taking it for a spin. Or—worst of all—we leave truth completely out of the picture.

6. Let's take some time now to reflect on specific relationships in your life. Prayerfully think through the people you encounter often, taking note of any with whom you seem to have a recurring problem of not being able to tell the truth. Write their name in the first column. Then, draw an arrow from their name in the first column to the reason you have this difficulty in the second column. Helping identify the reasons why you do not speak the entire truth is the first step in remedying this behavior.

PERSON	REASON
	I fear hurting their feelings.
	I am afraid of disappointing them.
	I want them to like me.
	I feel peer pressure to lie since no one else is telling them the truth.
	I've been doing it for so long that it is now a pattern.
	I am afraid of their reaction being one of anger or retaliation.
	Other: _____ (fill in the blank)

* IMPORTANT NOTE: This book was written with the average person in mind who deals with the normal feelings and pressure to please others. If you are dealing with a more serious issue such as verbal abuse or actual physical harm, get help! Reach out to your pastor, if you have one. Or you can find a Christian counselor in your area by visiting ccn.thedirectorywidget.com. Or, if you are in physical danger and being abused, please stop what you are doing now and call the National Domestic Abuse Hotline at 1-800-799-7233 or visit http://www.thehotline.org/

7. In the group time for this session, we took a deep dive into Proverbs 15:1: "A gentle answer turns away wrath, but a harsh word stirs up anger." Giving a truthful, but gentle, answer is the best policy when being asked for one's opinion. For many, this is quite a struggle. However, if we are armed with some premade responses that begin with a truthful and gentle sentence, it will help us in our relationships.

Here are a few go-to introductory sentences that may help you to share truthfully with someone in your life:

- I fear there being any awkwardness between us, but you deserve to know my honest thoughts, so I will give them to you.
- I know this might be hard to hear, but if the roles were reversed, I would want you to shoot straight with me.

- I know you are asking my honest opinion, so even though it might sting a little, I will honor your wishes and give it to you.
- I almost hesitate to tell my true thoughts because I care about you deeply and don't want to hurt your feelings.
- I value our friendship enough to not try to dress up the truth but share my thoughts honestly.

Which one of the above five sentences do you wish you would have been equipped with in a prior situation or which one might you use in the future and why? Place a star in front of it and then write your answer here.

While gossip can be defined as saying something behind someone's back that you'd never say to their face, flattery is much the reverse. It is uttering words to someone's face that you'd never say behind their back because they are totally untrue.

When Making Others Happy Is Making You Miserable, page 66

8. Read the following verses and passages. As you do, in the space beside them, record any words or phrases contained in them that showcase what our speech should be like and how we are to treat others.

PASSAGE	DESIRED BEHAVIOR
Proverbs 12:22	
Exodus 20:16	
Luke 6:31	
1 Corinthians 13:4–6	
2 Corinthians 8:21	
1 Peter 3:10–12	
1 John 3:18	

Now, using the words and phrases you wrote above, craft a sentence or two that sum up what our behavior should be like when interacting with others, specifically when it comes to pleasing God and loving people.

Scripture Memory Verse Reminder

Here again is our verse for this week. Take a little time to rehearse it aloud and commit it to memory to help you in your quest to be a truth teller who is also thoughtful and considerate.

"And stop lying to each other. You have given up your old way of life with its habits." (Colossians 3:9 CEV)

Session Four

You're Capable, but Are You Called?

We have passed the halfway mark of our study and it is now time for session four. During our time together, we will be looking at the many demands placed upon us due to both the devices and the people in our lives. So often we allow our schedules to be dictated by others who want to fill our time for us. It's time we allowed God to plan out our days instead. Let's get started exploring this very important concept.

Karen

In-Between Sessions Review (10 MINUTES)

Spend 10 minutes allowing group members to share what they most got out of the in-between sessions work since the last time you met. Was there a section of the book that really helped you? Perhaps a certain Scripture spoke to your soul? Maybe one of the questions was especially relevant to you right now in your season of life. Spend time discussing this before watching the session four video.

Video: You May be Capable, but Are You Called? (21 MINUTES)

Notes

The dawn of the digital age has completely revolutionized how we do life. Dozens of people can attempt to place tasks on our plates for us to do before getting any input—or approval—from us.

If you aren't intentional to fill your time, there are dozens of people out there waiting to fill it for you.

James 1:2–8 speaks about trials, sometimes translated as temptations. The Greek word for this concept used in the passage is *peirasmos*. It means a time of calamity that is unpleasant. But it can also mean a test—as in time of proving. But the most interesting parallel definition means an enticement or temptation.

Proverbs 29:25 revealed that the fear of humans is a snare. The Hebrew word, much like the Greek word in James 1:2–8, also conveys the concept of bait or a lure; something that is so enticing it may cause a person to put themselves in a place of danger.

Remind yourself that every need is not necessarily your call.

When you put some best digital practices in place, there's no doubt it will upset some people and you may have to navigate some uncomfortable conversations.

Realize that you can still say yes to a friendship without needing to say yes to that person's requests all the time.

Make it your aim to live a no-regret life.

As a guideline going forward that will help prevent you from becoming bogged down in too much activity or saying yes to too many commitments, tell yourself this:

Don't take on more than you can pray for.
Learn to say no; it will be of more use to you than to be able to read Latin.
—Charles Haddon Spurgeon

Group Discussion (25–35 MINUTES)

Take a few minutes to discuss what you just watched in the teaching video session.

1. In the teaching video, Karen asserted that the dawn of the digital age has completely revolutionized how we do life. What is your reaction to this statement? Can you think of any specific examples?

2. Can you think of any ways that devices and screens have personally cost you time or caused your plate to become too full?

3. God's Word has much to say about using our time wisely. Take turns having someone from your group read the following verses and passages aloud. As they are read, jot down any words or concepts that most stand out to you. Then, answer the questions that follow.

   - Psalm 90:12

   - Ephesians 5:15–17

   - 2 Corinthians 9:8

   - Colossians 4:5

- Proverbs 16:9

- James 4:13–14

Which of the above verses most spoke to your life right now and why?

Review the words and phrases you wrote down. Then, using a few of them, make a statement that indicates what God's Word says about how we spend our time.

4. After watching the teaching and listening to the verses from the last question, you may be desiring to make some changes in the way you handle your devices and screens. Brainstorm as a group any "screen time strategies" you might have. Think not only about limiting your usage of these devices, but also preventing other people from putting items on your plate through their connections with you digitally. See how many you can come up with. Here is one example:

> When it's time for me to sit down and focus on some paperwork, I will place my cell phone in the Do Not Disturb mode. This feature allows calls only from those on my "favorites list" and since I am the one who crafts this list, this will only allow immediate family to contact me and not everyone in my contact list.

Okay. Your turn! What are some screen time strategies you can implement?

8. When it comes to setting your schedule and using your time wisely, which of the following are most likely to trip you up because they take time or cause you to waste time? Name them and then tell the group why you chose the one (or ones) you did:

Children's activities   Friends who need help or want
Spouse's activities   my time
Social media interactions   Family members who need help or
Volunteer activities   want my time
Church or community responsibilities   Other _____ (fill in the blank)

9. Have someone read James 1:1–8 to the group. Then answer the questions below.

The Greek word for trials in verse two is *peirasmos*. It means a time of calamity that is unpleasant. However, it can also mean a test, as in time of proving. But the most interesting parallel definition means an enticement or temptation. What temptations do you face when dealing with the requests from people in your life, whether they come to you digitally or in person? Are you tempted to people-please? To take on too many responsibilities? To not be truthful? What temptations in this area do you experience?

Now, where in this same passage from James do we find the solution to facing these temptations? Give the verse or verses and tell what we are promised.

10. Have someone read Proverbs 29:25 to the group. A snare in the Old Testament culture wasn't just a trap. The Hebrew word also conveys the concept of bait or a lure; something that is so enticing it may cause someone to put themselves in a place of danger. The passage in James sheds further light on avoiding such trappings, temptations, and snares.

Using both the passage in James and the verse in Proverbs, take a few minutes to craft a prayer to God about dealing with the people and screens in your life, keeping in mind the promise given to us about wisdom in James. Once you are finished, see if anyone is willing to share their prayer with the group.

11. The Amplified Version (AMP) of Proverbs 15:23 reads:

> A man has joy in giving an appropriate answer,
> And how good and delightful is a word spoken at the right moment—
>> how good it is!

If our aim is to give an appropriate answer—which will ultimately bring joy, what have you learned from this session that can help you when it is time to answer a person who has a request of you? Rather than just making your decision based on what you know the other person wants to hear, what are some important guidelines to remember that will help you make a decision that is in keeping with God's Word?

12. BONUS QUESTION: Challenge time! Below are a few challenges. Some have to do with your phones or devices. Others have to do with the people in your life. Read through them and see if there are any you would like to take on as a personal challenge. After a few minutes to complete this exercise, see if any members want to share their goal.

Possible Challenges

- I will not keep my phone plugged in overnight in my bedroom but will place it in a different location of the house so I won't be tempted to tap and scroll, wasting time just before going to bed.
- I will learn to place my phone in the "Do Not Disturb" mode this week when I am having a meal with my family.
- I will limit my time on social media to 15 minutes per day.
- If anyone makes a request of me this week, I will not answer them for at least 24 hours until I have had time to pray about their ask.
- I will place a sticky note somewhere I will see often that reads: *Don't take on more than you can pray for.*
- (As an optional challenge, see if members would like to exchange contact information with someone else in the group who will check on them during the week to see how they are doing in the challenge they chose.)

Individual Activity: What Is God Asking Me to Do?

Complete this activity on your own.

Imagine your life as a plate, depicted in the graphic below. For each of the four quadrants, write down any ongoing commitments you have or tasks you have recently said yes to doing in that specific area. Once you're finished, prayerfully ask God if there's anything there that should be removed. Finally, write one action step you will take to begin to scrape off your too-full plate before placing back on it only the things you feel God calling you to do.

Action Step I Will Take:

_____

_____

_____

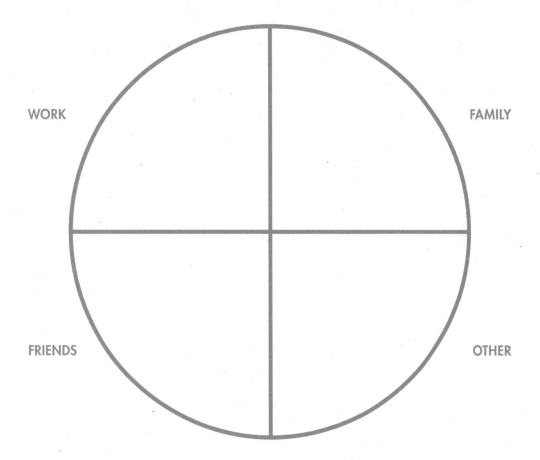

Session Four Memory Verse

As a group, practice saying this session's memory verse aloud together.

> "If any of you lacks wisdom, you should ask God, who gives generously to all without finding fault, and it will be given to you." (James 1:5)

Closing Prayer

Have one person close in prayer, focusing on your group's desire to not allow the pull of people and the tug of the phone to dictate your schedules, but rather allow the Lord to set your agendas. Then, get ready to learn more in your between-sessions personal study before meeting for lesson five!

Session Four

Between-Sessions Personal Study

"If any of you lacks wisdom, you should ask God, who gives generously to all without finding fault, and it will be given to you." (James 1:5)

Read Along and Learn

In the book *When Making Others Happy Is Making You Miserable*, read chapters 5–6. Use the space below to record any insights you discovered or questions you may want to bring to the next group session.

What stood out to me in chapter 5:

What I discovered or had thoughts about in chapter 6:

Study and Reflect

1. Flip back over the pages of notes from the video teaching and the group discussion time. What most stood out to you? Was it a particular exercise? The Greek or Hebrew meaning of a certain word? Was it something one of the group members said? Or was it one of the challenges issued? Write it down here.

2. In this session, we talked about how our devices can often steal our time and how people can digitally place items on our to-do list without any input or approval from us. How big of a problem do you think this is in your life? For each issue listed below, circle the phrase that best describes your situation.

Dealing with my devices is:

Not a problem at all   Barely problematic   Somewhat troublesome   Mostly problematic HELP!!!

Dealing with the requests from my people is:

Not a problem at all   Barely problematic   Somewhat troublesome   Mostly problematic HELP!!!

Now, choose either your people or your devices and write one change below that you wish to see happen in this area.

People assume you are tethered to your phone, having it always on your person. They expect you to instantly respond to any messages they might send you, whether by text or otherwise. Perhaps their expectations in this realm are due to the fact that they themselves are never without their phones. Their life is characterized by a constant interaction with their device. So, they find it quite strange when you do not conduct yourself the same way.

When Making Others Happy Is Making You Miserable, page 85

3. Let's take a trip back to the Old Testament where we are going to look at one of the most well-known characters of the Bible—Moses. And we are going to look at an entire chapter of the Bible—Exodus 18. Read it thorough once at a normal reading pace. Then, refer back to it to answer the questions below.

In a sentence or two, state what was Moses's dilemma? Give verses for your answers.

When Moses's father-in-law, Jethro, watched what was happening in the life of his son-in-law, he summed up his thoughts regarding Moses's behavior in a single phrase in verse 17. What did he say?

How would you use your own words to describe why the way Moses was handling things "was not good"? (NIV)

In the original Hebrew language, the word we get here translated as *good* is *towb*, meaning "pleasant, agreeable, and beneficial." Circle those three words and keep them in mind as you answer more about this topic in the next two questions.

In a nutshell, what was Jethro's solution for Moses. Write it here.

Finally, what were the results when Moses took his father-in-law's advice?

4. Have you ever found yourself in a situation in which you, like Moses, seem to be getting requests and interruptions all day long? Maybe it was in your job. Perhaps instead it was from your friends, especially on social media. It might even be from the requests of your family members throughout your day. Briefly describe the situation below.

What might you learn from Moses's narrative that you could apply to your situation? Is there something you need to delegate? Is there a way to more adequately handle the many requests that come your way so they do not stress you out and render you ineffective as a believer? What solutions can you think of?

5. Now, look back at the three words you circled in question three. Write them here.

Using these three words—*pleasant, agreeable,* and *beneficial*—examine your own schedule as it relates to the tasks and responsibilities others expect you to carry out. Would you say that, overall, your life in this area is pleasant, agreeable, and beneficial—not just to you, but to your family, who are often affected by your time-management decisions? Circle your answer below.

Yes   Somewhat   Not really   No way

What changes would you like to see made in this area?

Psalm 55 is thought by most Bible scholars to be penned by David, who wrote it while trying to escape a constant and treacherous enemy. Many times, we feel that the demands of life placed on us by other people are a constant enemy. Using Psalm 55:16–18, write a one-sentence prayer to God about the progress you would like to see made.

God's answer to you may be found as we read further in Psalm 55 and see what David says about the Lord rescuing him. What does Psalm 55:22 say? Copy it word for word here.

If God was faithful to rescue David, he will be faithful to rescue you! Circle the words you copied from verse 22 that you most need now in your life.

6. Psalm 31 was also written by David. Originally composed for the director of music, it has much to say to us today. Read it now, paying close attention to verses 14–15. Then read and answer the questions below.

While the psalmist David was talking about human enemies—those who could pursue, capture, and eventually hurt him—sometimes we look at our schedules and feel we are being hounded as well. So many people are putting pressure on us, or our many activities, tasks, and responsibilities are about to do us in. They chase us, corner us and—worst of all—we feel they are about to go in for the kill.

We've already talked about the tasks, responsibilities, and activities of your life. But let's use this time to narrow it down to the most concerning one. Which one do you feel most chased and hemmed in by?

Now, glance again at Psalm 31:14–15:

> ¹⁴ But I trust in you, Lᴏʀᴅ;
>> I say, "You are my God."
> ¹⁵ My times are in your hands;
>> deliver me from the hands of my enemies,
>> from those who pursue me.

Finally, turn this passage into your personal prayer, filling in the missing words below as you pray this Scripture aloud to God.

> ¹⁴·But I _____ in you, _____;
>> I say, "____ ____ ____ _____"
> ¹⁵ ____ _____ are in _____ _____;
>> _____ me from the _____ of my _____,
>> from those who _____ me.

Sticking to your guns and remaining consistent will take focused discipline. And loads of wisdom. And perpetual perseverance. But God is more than willing to give us all of this. Just remember, you don't owe others an excuse for why you said no, but you will owe God an explanation for why you said yes.

When Making Others Happy Is Making You Miserable, page 114

7. Prayer wasn't only for Bible characters such as David. It is a crucial part of learning to get our schedules under control. Do you make it a habit to pray about your schedule and the task and responsibilities you say yes to? If not, why do you think this is so?

Read through the following verses on prayer. In the line after each reference, write one fact about prayer that you glean from the verse.

VERSE	FACT ABOUT PRAYER
1 Thessalonians 5:16–18	
1 John 5:14–15	
Romans 12:12	
Hebrews 4:16	
Psalm 18:6	
Psalm 5:3	

8. What are your thoughts about the concept of living a no-regret life?

Karen gave an example from her life about choosing between two commitments/activities by asking herself which is the best choice if she wants to live a no-regret life. Can you think of some examples from your life?

Scripture Memory Verse Reminder

Here again is our verse for this week. Spend a little time trying to internalize and memorize it.

"If any of you lacks wisdom, you should ask God, who gives generously to all without finding fault, and it will be given to you." (James 1:5)

Session Five

Must Be Nice

Session Five Memory Verse
*He said to them, "Come away by yourselves to a remote place
and rest for a while." For many people were coming and going,
and they did not even have time to eat. (Mark 6:31 CSB)*

Welcome to session five of our study. In our time together, we will be exploring the concept of being nice. Is "niceness" something God calls us to? And is our quest to be nice costing us precious time that we could be using instead to rest and retreat, connecting our hearts to the heart of God. Let's see what treasures his word has for us in today's session.

Karen

In-Between Sessions Review (10 MINUTES)

Spend 10 minutes allowing group members to share what each got out of the in-between sessions work since the last time you were together. Was there a new concept or understanding of Scripture you learned? A reflection question you found challenging? A confirmation you had about your need to alter your behavior? Spend time discussing this before watching the session five video.

Video: Must Be Nice (21 MINUTES)

Play the video teaching segment for session five. As you watch, record any thoughts or concepts that stand out to you in the outline that follows.

Notes

A quick online search of the three translations Karen uses most often when studying and teaching the Bible—the ESV, CSB, and NIV versions—yielded not one solitary result when searching for the word *nice*.

Research concludes that often we go along to get along, being overly nice simply to avoid mental stress. However, what we often don't realize is that our being extremely nice may cause us greater mental stress in the future than it would in the present moment.

If we want to prevent the unpleasant fallout from being too nice, we need to enact some relational boundaries.

Boundaries are a blessing. Put them in place and watch them work. Your relationships will be healthier in the long run.

In Mark 6:31, in the Amplified Version, we read:

> He said to them, "Come away by yourselves to a secluded place and rest a little while"—for there were many [people who were continually] coming and going, and they could not even find time to eat.

The Greek word from which we get the English word *come* means "to come hither." The simple definition of *hither* is "to or toward."

The word translated into English as *away* has a variety of meanings, including "after, down from (as in 'to a lower place'), face to face, in the presence of, and privately."

The original Greek phrase that translates to the English "by yourselves" means "you, all alone, to the exclusion of others." It also means "prompted or influenced by another, but of one's own accord."

The word *place* in Greek does mean "location, region, or seat." However, it also can be used to signify an opportunity.

The writer of Psalm 62:5 tells us how to remedy our worn-out souls: "Rest in God alone." The word *alone* has an insightful Hebrew meaning here: "in stark contrast to any other ideas; the only solution that works; the real one rather than a counterfeit."

If you don't take some time for your relationship with your heavenly Father, your earthly relationships will suffer.

You teach people how to treat you by what you allow, what you stop, and what you reinforce.
—Tony Gaskins Jr.

Group Discussion (25–35 MINUTES)

Take a few minutes to discuss what you just watched in the teaching video session.

1. What are your thoughts about the revelation that the word *nice* is not found in Scripture, and that Jesus never commanded his followers to be nice?

2. What do you think the difference is between nice and kind? How might we mix up the meanings of these two words?

3. What are your thoughts on the research Karen cited about what happens in our brains when we speak something to another person that we know they will find unpleasant or which might even anger them? Can you cite any specific instances of this happening to you personally?

4. It can feel strange to put ourselves first. It may seem selfish or even unchristian. However, we aren't talking about frivolous time alone. We are talking about times of quiet with a spiritual purpose—to grow closer to God and refresh our souls. What do you think is your greatest hindrance in life right now when it comes to carving out some time to meet with God?

Can you think of a time when you did find margin in your day to spend some uninterrupted time studying the Bible, journaling, praying, or worshiping God alone? Tell the group about that time and what it meant to you.

5. Look back over the notes you took during the teaching session. Specifically, glance at what you wrote about Jesus's words in Mark 6:31. Which explanation of the following Greek words did you find most interesting and why?

- *Come:* means "to come hither." The simple definition of *hither* is "to or toward."
- *Away:* means "after, down from (as in 'to a lower place'), face to face, in the presence of, and privately."
- *By yourselves:* means "you, all alone, to the exclusion of others." It also means "prompted or influenced by another, but of one's own accord."
- *Place:* means "location, region, or seat." However, it also can be used to signify an opportunity.

Has this deeper look into Mark 6:31 made you want to change anything in the future as it relates to spending time alone with God?

6. Take turns having one person in your group read aloud each of the following verses. Then, answer the question that follows.

   Leviticus 23:3
   Exodus 34:21
   Exodus 33:14
   Hebrews 4:9

These verses referred to the Old Testament practice of the Jews observing the Sabbath. Even though we are not under the Old Testament law anymore, many believers still observe a weekly day of rest.

For the Jews, they rested on the seventh day of the week, which is Saturday. The early Christian church instead switched this to the first day of the week, Sunday, because Jesus rose from the dead on the first day of the week and therefore it became known as the Lord's Day. Still other Christians have to work on the day their church body observes the Sabbath, so they take a Sabbath on their day off from work during the week.

Do you observe the practice of a weekly Sabbath day to rest from work? If so, how do you spend it? Do you have any particular traditions or habits associated with this day?

7. Below are some verses that speak to individual rest and quiet. Have them read aloud by various group members. As they are read, place a star beside any that are particularly meaningful to you, writing down any words that stand out as you listen. Afterward, answer the question below.

    Psalm 116:7
    Psalm 4:8
    Psalm 127:2
    Psalm 37:7
    Ecclesiastes 4:6
    Matthew 11:28
    Psalm 46:10

Which verse or verses did you star? What are the words or phrases you found meaningful in those Scriptures? How do you think the verse or verses that you chose speaks to your life at the current time?

8. In our quest to find rest and quiet—making meeting with God a priority—we will have to put some boundaries in place with the people in our lives. Also, we will need to adopt some daily practices that free up time in our schedules. If we allow everyone else to fill our time, we won't have any time left for God. If we don't earnestly create space in our calendars for an appointment with God—just like any other important appointment we might have in life—it simply won't get done.

Do you currently have any boundaries with people in your life that enable you to carve out time to meet with God? If so, what are they? (Example: Your children know that every evening at 7 o'clock you spend 15 minutes reading the Bible and then 15 minutes going on a prayer walk. They know that—unless there is an emergency—they are not to bother you during that time.)

Now, let's talk about best practices. Do you have some habits and strategies that help create margin in your day so that you can spend time reading, praying, journaling, pondering, worshiping, or simply listening quietly before the Lord? Maybe you shut off your phone a half hour before bed and use the time to read your Bible and pray rather than tap, swipe, and scroll through social media. If you have a habit, practice, or strategy, share it with the group.

Psalm 119 is the longest psalm—and longest chapter—in the Bible. (Don't worry. We aren't going to attempt to cover it all!) Although his name is not in the intro to it, most scholars believe it to be written by David. Like Psalm 34 that we studied earlier, this too is an acrostic poem, in which each set of eight verses begins with a letter of the Hebrew alphabet. Have group members take turns reading Psalm 119:147–148 aloud in as many translations as you can find. Then, answer the question below.

What does this portion of Scripture say about seeking the Lord and giving him the best part of your day? (NOTE: This is a no judgment zone. Not everyone can get up super early in the day. Due to work schedule, small children, or other such realities of life this just might not be possible for some

people. The point of this question is not about giving God an *early* time slot in your day, but rather about giving him the *best* part of your day, whenever you can arrange for a focused and uninterrupted time.)

Here is a challenge for your group. If you have any members who, due to caring for small children or even aging parents, have very little time to spend meeting with God alone, what are some ways you can rally around them? Can you have a few members volunteer to watch the kids one Saturday morning so a maxed-out mom might have a three-hour stretch alone with God? Can you take up a collection for a woman who is becoming emotionally and physically worn out from caring for a family member so she can go overnight to a bed and breakfast for some alone time? Prayerfully consider how you who have no trouble finding pockets of time to be alone can assist those whose lives do not currently afford such luxury.

9. BONUS QUESTION: The psalmist David tells us in Psalm 62:5 how to remedy our worn-out souls: "Rest in God alone." The word *alone* in this verse has an insightful Hebrew meaning here. It is "in stark contrast to any other ideas; the only solution that works; the real one rather than a counterfeit." We don't always look to God alone for our rest. We look other places and to other people. What are some other counterfeit ways we try to seek rest, quiet, and retreat in our lives? List them here.

Now, for each one of those counterfeit ways, explain why they do not work. Why is God the only place to find true rest? Have you ever discovered this reality for yourself and, if so, what happened?

10. BONUS QUESTION: Time to talk progress. You've now been through five sessions of *When Making Others Happy Is Making You Miserable.* What has been the greatest takeaway from the study thus far? And secondly, in what way has it caused you to want to change your thinking on this subject? Here is an example:

> Perhaps you especially liked learning that every need is not necessarily your call. Before, you always felt your heart being tugged at whenever you heard of a need. Therefore, you wrongly concluded that you were the person to meet such needs every time. But now you want to change your thinking. Going forward, when you hear of a need, you plan to remind yourself that it might not be your call and you need to pause, ponder, and pray before volunteering to help be part of the solution.

Your turn! Record your greatest takeaway and your changed thinking patterns in the spaces below. Then, allow any group members who would like to share their answer out loud to do so.

Biggest takeaway so far:

Change in thinking I want to make:

Individual Activity: What Is God Asking Me to Do?

Complete this activity on your own.

Take a moment to get alone in your thoughts, quiet before the Lord. Take an honest assessment of how well you build into your daily life the practice of resting from your responsibilities to connect with God. What grade would you give yourself?

Grade: _____

What is one action step you can take to more consistently carve out time to meet with God and rest in his presence so you don't let the pull of people overwhelm you? Write that action step out below.

_____

_____

_____

Session Five Memory Verse

He said to them, "Come away by yourselves to a remote place and rest for a while." For many people were coming and going, and they did not even have time to eat. (Mark 6:31 CSB)

Closing Prayer

Have one person close in prayer, focusing on your group's desire to make spending time alone with God a regular life practice. Then, get ready to learn more in your between-sessions personal study before meeting for our final time together!

Between-Sessions Personal Study

He said to them, "Come away by yourselves to a remote place and rest for a while." For many people were coming and going, and they did not even have time to eat. (Mark 6:31 CSB)

Read Along and Learn

Read chapter 7 of When Making Others Happy Is Making You Miserable. *Use the space below to record any insights you discovered or questions you may want to bring to the next group session.*

Study and Reflect

1. Review what you wrote down in your study guide during your group time for this session. What overall concept was your favorite? Which Scripture portion or word meaning did you find most helpful? Do you plan to make any adjustments in your thinking or behavior in the future because of what you learned?

2. If someone were to look at your life with regard to how you spend your waking hours, would they conclude that spending time alone with God is a high priority for you? What solid evidence—or lack thereof—is there in your behavior that shows how important you think this practice is?

3. Perhaps one of the most well-known twosomes in the Bible are the New Testament sisters Mary and Martha. We meet them several places in Scripture. For now, let's just focus on what we see happening between them and Jesus in Luke 10:38–42. Read that passage and then answer the questions that follow.

First, let's set up the scene. In your own words, describe what was happening in this passage.

As you look at what is written about each sister in this passage, what adjectives might you give to describe them? Write those descriptive words in the space after each of their names.

Martha: _____

Mary: _____

Luke 10: 38–42 (ESV) says this about the sisters: ". . . but one thing is necessary. Mary has chosen the good portion, which will not be taken away from her." In various Bible translations, "the good portion" is instead called "the good part," "the right choice," or "what is better."

In the original Greek, this phrase is composed of two words. The first word is *agathos* and it means "intrinsically good, good in nature, good whether it be seen to be so or not." The second word is *meris* and it means "portion, part, district, or share."

What do you find interesting about the original meaning of these two words that make up this phrase, rendered in various ways in the English?

How can choosing "the good portion" today keep us from worry, being troubled, and pleasing others at the detriment to our own future peace of mind?

When we repeatedly give in to the wishes of others—without ever sharing our true feelings or standing up for ourselves—we teach them how to treat us, paving the way for their future bad behavior.

When Making Others Happy Is Making You Miserable, page 122

4. We also find the concept of resting and quieting ourselves so we can hear from the Lord in the Old Testament. Elijah was one of the most important and most respected prophets in Israel's history. God used him to bring about a revival in the Northern Kingdom and accomplished a number of miracles through him.

King Ahab and Queen Jezebel were Elijah's greatest earthly enemies during his life. King Ahab and the prophets met Elijah on Mount Carmel where they performed a contest to see who had the strongest god. Baal's priests lost the competition, and they were slaughtered by the people. King Ahab was furious, and Jezebel wanted to annihilate Elijah for the injury that he had done to her fabricated religious system. As a result, Elijah had to flee into the wilderness.

Let's pick up the story by reading 1 Kings 19:1–18. Then, answer the questions below.

When the prophet Elijah ran away, he grew very discouraged. He even gave a rather strange prayer request to God. What did he pray for in verse 4?

God sent provisions for the prophet in the form of an angel. What did the angel encourage Elijah to do?

Strengthened by these provisions, Elijah traveled to Horeb, the mountain of God. He was told that the Lord would pass by. Then, four different events took place. Write them in the order they appear in verses 11–13.

- _____
- _____
- _____
- _____

In which event did Elijah finally hear from the Lord?

What conditions are necessary for a whisper to be heard?

What did Elijah immediately do when he finally heard the voice of God in the whisper?

5. Let's think about your life for a moment. We all have people, situations, tasks, and responsibilities clamoring for our attention. There are events in our lives that threaten to blow us over like a mighty wind, wreaking havoc on our circumstances. Sometimes we may feel like we are in the middle of a relational earthquake. We might be walking through a medical situation that feels like a blazing fire. But if we, like Elijah, want to hear God's whispers to us—that come through his Holy Word—we need to quiet down long enough to listen and learn.

Take a few minutes in the space below to pour out your heart to God on this matter. Have you allowed the clamor of life to drown out his Word? Has he been whispering but you have been too busy—or too uninterested—to hear? Tell Jesus your honest thoughts and ask him to help you listen more closely going forward.

6. Look up the following verses in the book of Psalms. Then answer the questions below.

    Psalm 27:8
    Psalm 63:1
    Psalm 119:2

What word do all the above verses have in common?

In Hebrew, the word for *seek* is *baqash*. It means more than just to look for. This multi-layered word also means "to pursue, consult, request, plead" and even "to beg." How does learning the deeper meaning of this Hebrew word change how you will approach the Lord in your prayer time in the future?

7. Now, read the following verses, also found in Psalms. Then answer the questions below.

> Psalm 130:5
> Psalm 40:1
> Psalm 27:14
> Psalm 37:7

What word do all these Scriptures have in common?

The Hebrew word for *wait* is *qavah*. It means more than just drumming your fingers and passing the time. It more literally means "to linger, remain, endure, and look eagerly for." It is an anticipatory longing that is confident in the answer to come. How does learning the deeper meaning of this Hebrew word change how you will behave after your prayer time in the future?

So, when our souls are siphoned due to the draining duties of our roles, or our overcommitment due to people pleasing, we have a guaranteed remedy. And it isn't a nap or a break from our responsibilities—though those things can play a part. The cure is God, who alone can soothe and satisfy our souls.

When Making Others Happy Is Making You Miserable, page 139

8. Jesus himself found it important to get away for a while; to slow down and cease activity. He also urged his disciples to get to a quiet place (Mark 6:31). In doing so they would find rest. Being alone and quiet would help keep them whole.

In our fast-paced society we rarely get to sit still in a quiet space. Music blasts. Streaming services shout. Computers broadcast our online meetings. Our phones crank out social media posts at times when we could be seeking solace. As a result, stress chisels away, creating small cracks in our souls that—no matter how tiny— could cause us to shatter under the heat and pressures of everyday life.

Let's purpose to take time this week to slow down, get away, and rest. To find solitude in a hushed and holy place alone with our Savior, even if only for an hour or two.

Grab your calendar—whether it is of paper or the digital sort. Look over your next week or two. Do you see even a one-hour stretch where you could get alone to be with Jesus? Log this appointment with him in now. And then? Make sure to keep it. Yes, it may require some rearranging. You may need to hire a sitter or have a friend or family member watch the kiddos for you. But the siphoning of your soul needs to stop. It is time to rest in God alone.

Use the space provided here to also record when and where you will meet with Jesus.

Now, what tools and resources will you bring with you? Besides your Bible, is there a devotional or theological book that might be helpful in facilitating this time with God? How about a journal to record your deepest prayers and to chronicle your gratefulness to God? Will you create a playlist of worship songs to end your time with praise? What will you bring to this important meeting with the Lord?

Now, read aloud Psalm 17:6–8, making it your personal and heartfelt petition to the Father.

> ⁶ I call on you, my God, for you will answer me;
>
> turn your ear to me and hear my prayer.
>
> ⁷ Show me the wonders of your great love,
>
> you who save by your right hand
>
> those who take refuge in you from their foes.
>
> ⁸ Keep me as the apple of your eye;
>
> hide me in the shadow of your wings

Scripture Memory Verse Reminder

Here again is our verse for this session. Spend a few moments pondering it and trying to commit it to memory.

He said to them, "Come away by yourselves to a remote place and rest for a while." For many people were coming and going, and they did not even have time to eat. (Mark 6:31 CSB)

Session Six

Your People and Your Punch List

Session Six Memory Verse

I love those who love me; And those who seek me early
and diligently will find me. (Proverbs 8:17 AMP)

The time has come for our very last session of *When Making Others Happy Is Making You Miserable*. This gathering is all about learning to manage the time we allot to our relationships and our responsibilities. We will do this by examining the only person to ever do this perfectly—Jesus himself. Are you ready? Let's finish strong by analyzing our people and our punch lists, both in our group time and in our final study time alone.

Karen

In-Between Sessions Review (10 MINUTES)

Spend 10 minutes allowing group members to share what each got out of the in-between sessions work since the last time you met. Was there something that challenged you? Did you learn something new? Did you feel convicted by something or had questions for the other group members? Spend time discussing this before watching the session six video.

Video: Your People and Your Punch List (20 MINUTES)

Play the video teaching segment for session six. As you watch, record any thoughts or concepts that stand out to you in the outline that follows.

Notes

A look at how we spend our time will tell us if we are living our priorities.

Jesus had a packed agenda while on earth, peppered with both people and purpose.

The Lord remained consistent in his calling and yet confident in his human interactions, knowing when to pour into others and when to withdraw to rest.

People pleasing can sometimes be steeped in pride.

According to Proverbs 11:2, "When pride comes, then comes disgrace, but with humility comes wisdom." The Hebrew word for *disgrace* means "reproach, dishonor, and shame."

Our pride makes us behave certain ways to maintain our reputation of being capable, competent, or compassionate. If we aren't careful, our behavior can border on idolatry. We are worshiping an image—our own!

The more deliberate you want to be with your time—and the greater your desire to please God with your schedule—the more people you must be willing to disappoint.

You and I can determine to confidently live a no-regret life starting right now.

Spotted on a coffee mug:
"I am a recovering people pleaser. Is that all right with you?"

Group Discussion (25–35 MINUTES)

Take a few minutes to discuss what you just watched in the teaching video session.

1. In the video teaching for this session, Karen asserted that Jesus lived his priorities. He stayed consistent in his calling and yet confident in his human interactions, knowing when to pour into others and when to withdraw to rest. How does this encourage or challenge you?

2. Can you think of someone who you believe lives their priorities well? This would be a person who devotes their attention to the people and things in their life that need it, but who also knows their limitations and says no to others when they should. Describe that person and why you chose them.

3. No matter our stage of life, we have people and we also have a punch list. We are constantly navigating our days knowing there are persons and projects that need our attention. Which would you say is more typical of you—that you tend to put projects over people or people over projects? Or, does it depend on the situation? Share with your group your thoughts on tending to both your relationships and your responsibilities.

4. Like us, Jesus had numerous individuals in his life. He also had to decide to what and to whom he would devote his time each day. Look up the following verses and in the blanks after them, list the various people with whom Jesus interacted.

Matthew 5:1; 7:28–8:1; 14:13–14	
Mark 5:22–35	
Matthew 13:55–56	
Luke 1:35–38; 57–60	
Luke 10:1–3	
Matthew 10:1–5; Mark 10:32–34	
Matthew 17:1–3; Mark 14:32–34; Luke 8:51	

Jesus spent time with the crowds. He sometimes hung out with his twelve closet companions. And on some occasions, he was deliberate to fix his focus on one single soul. He had family members who needed his attention. And he even had a tight circle of friends that included just three. You are no different. You must manage the tension between centering your time on a few or a crowd; between hanging out with friends or focusing on family.

How does knowing that Jesus had to navigate all these relationships encourage you? Is there anything you observe from how he interacted with others that might help us today?

5. In the video, the topics of pride and idolatry were not only discussed, but they were also tethered to each other. Do you think that sometimes pride is involved when we people-please? Why or why not?

When we are too prideful to be honest with others—or we let our pride cause us to take on too many responsibilities—Karen asserted that we are fiercely trying to bolster, maintain, or protect our image. When our image is what is most important to us, it becomes image worship, which is a form of idolatry. Is this a new concept to you? What danger is there in caring more about our image than we do about God?

6. The Bible has many warnings to us about allowing pride to creep into our hearts and come out in our behavior. Theologian C. S. Lewis once claimed, "Pride leads to every other vice: it is the complete anti-God state of mind."*

Take turns having someone from the group read each of these verses aloud. As you do, fill in the blanks in the spaces after each verse about what pride is and what the opposite of pride is. Not each verse will have items in both columns, but some will.

---

*   https://merecslewis.blogspot.com/2011/11/pride-leads-to-every-other-vice.html

REFERENCE	PRIDE IS	THE OPPOSITE OF PRIDE IS
Psalm 138:6		
Psalm 31:23		
Proverbs 11:2		
Proverbs 16:18		
Proverbs 29:23		
Isaiah 66:2		
Luke 14:11		
James 4:6		

After scrutinizing all these verses on pride, how would you explain to someone why pride is dangerous and a slippery slope?

Also based on what you read in these verses, what would you say is the opposite of pride? Why can't both pride and its opposite coexist in a person's behavior?

7. If we have our priorities in order, we will love and serve God above all without neglecting to love others. If God calls us to both please him and love others, he will provide us with all we need to carry out these two calls. What do the following verses tell us about loving others while also pleasing God? Have one person from the group read a verse. After each one is read, have members chime in on what actions and attitudes we must have in order to properly love others while we purpose to please God.

Colossians 3:12

Ephesians 4:2

Micah 6:8

Matthew 22:37–39

John 13:34

John 14:23–24

8. In the teaching for this session, Karen stated: *The more deliberate you want to be with your time—and the greater your desire to please God with your schedule—the more people you must be willing to disappoint.* Is this a new thought for you or have you found this to be true in your life? If this is something you've experienced, please share your experience with the group.

9. BONUS QUESTION: Here are some go-to phrases from the book *When Making Others Happy Is Making You Miserable* that will help you realign your thinking when you start to wander down the path of people pleasing.

    Which one or two do you most need to remember or apply in your relationships in the future? Doing so can help you to not put people in the place of God but confidently live your life according to his ways.

    - **Every need is not necessarily your call.**
    - **Don't take on more than you can pray for.**
    - **Their happiness is not your assignment.**
    - **You don't need their permission to do God's will.**
    - **Stop making their feelings your responsibility.**
    - **You don't owe them an excuse for why you said no, but you will owe God an explanation for why you said yes.**
    - **You can still say yes to the friendship while saying no to a friend.**

10. BONUS QUESTION: When you ponder what you have learned over the course of these six sessions together, what would you say is your greatest takeaway or one practice you want to implement going forward?

Individual Activity: What Is God Asking Me to Do?

Complete this activity on your own.

Take a moment to reflect on your life when it comes to the trap of people pleasing. This study was designed most importantly to help you understand the proper fear of the Lord and stop giving in to the fear of humans. Have you made progress in this area? In the space below, complete the thoughts, using your own words. Then spend a minute or two making your aim a matter of silent prayer before God.

I have learned from this study that people pleasing is _____.
I no longer want to be afraid to _____.
One adjustment I want to make in how I use my digital devices is _____.
One action step I want to take in dealing with the people in my life is _____
_____.

Session Six Memory Verse

Time for our final memory verse! As a group, read it out loud together:

> I love those who love me; And those who seek me early and diligently will find me.
> (Proverbs 8:17 AMP)

Closing Prayer

Have one person close in prayer, focusing on your group's desire to learn to implement what they have learned from God's Word during your six sessions together. Then, get ready for your final between-sessions personal study!

Session Six

Final Personal Study

Session Six Memory Verse

> I love those who love me; And those who seek me early and diligently will find me.
> (Proverbs 8:17 AMP)

Read Along and Learn

Read chapters 8–9 of When Making Others Happy Is Making You Miserable. *Use the space below to record any insights you discovered or questions you may want to ask your facilitator or other group member.*

What I discovered or had thoughts about in chapter 8:

The highlights or questions for me from chapter 9 are:

Study and Reflect

1. Flip back over the pages of notes from the video teaching and the group discussion time. Did you have a favorite part? Was a particular exercise eye-opening? Did one of the verses you studied prove to be especially helpful? Write it down here.

2. Let's talk priorities for a moment. If someone were to ask you to list your priorities, most likely you would put God first, your close family members second, followed by work, friends, and so on down the list. However, often the reality of our behavior—how we spend our time and where we focus our energies—depicts quite a different scenario.

   Fill in the following list with the people, tasks, and responsibilities you have, ranking them in order of greatest priority. Don't forget to include your relationship with God. If you need more blanks, draw them in yourself underneath the chart.

MY PRIORITIES

1.
2.
3.
4.
5.
6.
7.
8.
9.
10.

Take an honest glance at the list you have constructed. How well are what you claim to be your top priorities lining up with how you spend your time? Of course, you can't determine this merely by the number of minutes or hours you spend with each one. If you must put in 40 hours a week at a job, you don't have any wiggle room on that. Pay closer attention to the amount of focus, energy, and prayer you place on each one and how attentive you are to the needs and feelings of the people on the list. Does your list line up with how you spend your time?

- Review the list you generated. Underline any items that you believe are getting the proper measure of your focus, time, and energy.
- Next, circle any of the priorities that you feel are not getting the right amount of attention.
- Finally, place a star next to the one you most want to focus on improving in the coming weeks.

Why did you choose the one that you starred? What specifically would you like to see change when it comes to that priority in your life?

3. I find the Old Testament prophet Jeremiah rather fascinating. The son of a priest, he was from the tiny town of Anathoth in Judah (Jeremiah 1:1). Jeremiah spent his adult years dictating prophecies from God to his personal assistant, Baruch (Jeremiah 36:4). The account of Jeremiah gives us a peek into the life of this servant. The glimpse we receive shows not merely a prophet who delivers God's message but also as a compassionate man who cared about others. In fact, he is sometimes labeled "The Weeping Prophet" because of his earnest and tender concern for his fellow humans. He successfully balanced serving God and loving people.

Interestingly, the account of Jeremiah also provides us a foreshadowing of the new covenant God will make with his people in the future when Christ is born. This new covenant would be the vehicle for redemption and eternal life for believers. God would put his law inside of his followers, inscribing it on hearts of flesh rather than chiseling it on tablets of stone (Jeremiah 31:33; 2 Corinthians 3:3).

No longer would people need to go to the temple to meet with the Lord. Instead, the account of Jeremiah shows that humans would come to know God directly through his only son, Jesus Christ (Jeremiah 31:31–34; Hebrews 8:6).

It can be such an encouragement when we see how the Lord dealt with his people on the pages of the Bible. And since the Lord God never changes (Malachi 3:6), we know he can still deal as mercifully and directly with us today as he did with the ancient prophets. We are going to take just three quick snapshots of the Lord interacting with Jeremiah.

Read each of the following verses or passages below. After each, answer the related questions.

First, read Jeremiah 32:26–27. How is God described in this passage?

When the word of the Lord came to Jeremiah, what question did God ask about himself?

How does knowing that the Lord is the God of all mankind encourage you?

Because God declared that nothing is too hard for him, there is no limit to the help he can offer us today when it comes to wanting to live a life pleasing him rather than pleasing people. What hard thing in this quest do you want to ask God to empower you to do? Write it in the space below.

Next, look up Jeremiah 33:1–3. Verse 1 of this chapter says that Jeremiah was confined in the courtyard of the guard. However, the word of the Lord came to him. How is the Lord described in this passage?

What promise does God speak to Jeremiah in verse 3? Write it out word for word in the space below.

God declared that he would answer. He promised to reveal great and unsearchable things that Jeremiah and the people did not know. He can do the same for us today. Maybe you *do not know* how you will ever break the pattern of people pleasing. Maybe you *do not know* how in the world you will find the courage to speak honestly when it would be so much easier to lie. Maybe you *do not know* how to manage the tension between your people and your punch list. But you, like Jeremiah, can call out to God. The Lord who made the earth will answer you.

In a few sentences, write out a prayer to the Lord asking him to equip you to do something you simply do not know how to do.

When we allow other people to determine the schedule we keep, we fail to honor God with the time that we have. And our souls are showing it—big time.

When Making Others Happy Is Making You Miserable, page 145

4. Just as God helped the people in Jeremiah's day not to fear but to forge forward, he
    can help us today. Change can be scary, and change is required if we want to alter
    our behavior to see that how we spend our time pleases God.

    Look up the following passages from the book of Psalms that use the word
    fear. After each, write the word or two that first popped into your mind when
    you read the verses. It may be an adjective or two that describes fear. Maybe
    it will be a phrase about a characteristic of God. Simply write down the first
    few words that come to mind about each verse or passage.

    Psalm 3:6

    Psalm 91:1–7

    Psalm 46:1–3

    Psalm 27:2–4

    Psalm 34:8–10

    X marks the spot! Based on the Scripture passages you just read, how are
    you doing when it comes to trusting God and not being afraid—particularly
    when it comes to fearing the opinions of others or making them unhappy
    with your words and actions? Place an X on the continuum below closest to
    where you would say your overall behavior falls:

I greatly fear the opinions of others, even over fearing the Lord.	I sometimes allow the fear of humans to prevail, but at other times rest secure, trusting in God.	I have the assurance that God is with me, so I typically fear him more than I fear the opinions of others.

Now, are there any adjustments you need to make to your behavior to align it more closely with the verses you studied above? If so, what are they?

5. You may be experiencing a little bit of anxiety when you think about altering your schedule and stopping the habit of saying yes to people all the time. You know there may be some awkwardness, or even some relational fallout. Time to calm our anxious fears!

Read Philippians 4:6–7 and then answer the questions below.

What is the first direction Paul gives to the church at Philippi in verse 6?

Does he give any leeway? Does he tell us that there are certain times that we *should* be anxious? Write the phrase that gives you your answer below. (Hint: It is also found in verse 6.)

When we do feel anxiety welling up, the apostle Paul gives us a solution, a tangible action to take, also found in verse 6. (Verse 6 is such a gold mine, right?) Fill in the blanks below that will help flush out this solution and cement it in your thinking. (To keep us on the same page, here is verse 6 in the New American Standard Bible [NASB] translation.)

Do not be anxious about anything, but in everything by prayer and pleading with thanksgiving let your requests be made known to God.

Now, fill in the missing blanks.

Do not be _____ about _____, but in _____ by _____ and _____ with _____ let your _____ be made known to _____.

You're not done yet! Is there a word that you placed in the blanks above that most resonates with you right now? If so, circle it. Then, in the space provided here, explain why you chose that word. Finally, use the word to write out a one- or two-sentence prayer to God about managing the tension between your people and your punch list.

At the end of our lives, we aren't going to be graded on how loud the crowds were roaring, cheering us on as we met their expectations. No. It all comes down to you and Jesus. He is the only one sitting in the bleachers. We are performing for an audience of one.

When Making Others Happy Is Making You Miserable, page XX

6. On pages 180–181 of *When Making Others Happy Is Making You Miserable*, Karen writes,

As someone who has struggled for decades with being controlled by the opinions and expectations of others, I also know it can be done. We learn to do it when we determine to discontinue our chant of can't.

I can't tell them the truth for risk of disappointing them.
I can't say no to their request because they are counting on me.

I can't stand up for myself, so I guess I will just acquiesce.
I can't guard my time, even though I know meeting their need is going to stress me right out.

Will you decide today to begin conquering your can't? God will provide the strength as you run to him rather than bow to others.

It's time to conquer YOUR can't. When it comes to breaking the pattern of people pleasing and confidently living your life for the glory of God—rather than for the approval of others—what "can'ts" do you have? Is there something you fear you can't do? Or is there an action you feel you can't *stop* doing? Write two or three of your apprehensions and fears in the blank spaces below.

I can't _____

I can't _____

I can't _____

Time to turn your worries into worship. Review the statements you just wrote and instead turn each of them into a worshipful declaration instead. For example, if you wrote:

I can't tell the truth to people for risk of disappointing them.

You will flip the script and declare:

Father, I praise you for granting me the strength and courage to be truthful with others while also being kind. Thank you for teaching me that the happiness of others does not depend solely on me. It is your job to bring them joy.

Okay. Now it is your turn. In the space below, flip your *"I can't"* into a *"he can!"*

7. These last several weeks have been full of discovery, sharing, and earnest requests for God's help. If you were to sum up in one paragraph what you have learned from this journey, what would you say? Specifically ponder how you want your thinking to change in the future or your behavior to modify when you deal with the topic of pleasing people.

8. Finally, don't let the truths you've explored in God's Word stay tucked in your Bible after this study is over. Take a few moments to flip back through this study guide. Are there any specific verses you found helpful or convicting? Was there a Bible character you loved learning about? Can you identify any key memory verses that you want to cling to in the future? List that information in the space below.

Now, grab your phone (or a paper calendar or planner if that's how you roll). Choose some random days over the next six months and type (or write down) each Scripture reference or Bible character. Then, when that day comes around, take just a few minutes to look up the verse or person to recall what you learned. Ready? Okay. Go ahead and flip, locate, and record these Scriptures and people in your calendar.

Scripture Memory Verse Reminder

Here again is our final memory verse:

I love those who love me; And those who seek me early and diligently will find me. (Proverbs 8:17 AMP)

A Final Word from Karen

I am so grateful that you spent time with us as we explored how to stop putting people in the place of God, living with full confidence in him instead. It has been my joy to help facilitate our study of Scripture—the place where we can discover godly answers to our earthly dilemmas. May the truths you've learned, the goals you've made, and the friendships you've forged assist you in your continual quest to please God, not people. Will you allow me the honor of praying for you?

Father, I pray for the person now reading this prayer. May they look to you alone for approval. May their thoughts and actions be in line with your Word. Empower them to resist the pressure to give in to the opinions and expectations of others. May they properly fear you and not allow the fear of humans to be a snare. Grant them peace in their soul and resolve in their mind as they live their life for an audience of One. In your precious Son's name, I pray. Amen.

Additional Resources

Here are seven "Stop It!" statements to use to remind yourself to not cave to the trap of people pleasing. You can photocopy this page, cutting out the statements and placing them where you are sure to see them often.

Every need
is not necessarily

YOUR CALL.

Don't take on

MORE THAN

you can

pray for.

Their

happiness

is not your

ASSIGNMENT.

You don't

need their

PERMISSION

to do

God's will.

Stop making

their

feelings

your

RESPONSIBILITY.

You don't owe them *an excuse* for why you SAID NO, but you will *owe God* an explanation for why you SAID YES.

You can still

SAY YES

to the

friendship

while saying no

TO A FRIEND.

Scripture Memory Verses

Each session includes a key Scripture verse that highlights the main topic. If you wish to maximize your learning experience, you may want to attempt to memorize these verses. To assist you with this goal, here are all six verses printed out for you. You may photocopy this page on paper or card stock and then cut the verses out.

Session 1

Am I now trying to win the approval of human beings, or of God? Or am I trying to please people? If I were still trying to please people, I would not be a servant of Christ.
Galatians 1:10 (NIV)

Session 2

On the contrary, we speak as those approved by God to be entrusted with the gospel. We are not trying to please people but God, who tests our hearts.
1 Thessalonians 2:4 (NIV)

Session 3

And stop lying to each other. You have given up your old way of life with its habits.

Colossians 3:9 (CEV)

Session 4

If any of you lacks wisdom, you should ask God, who gives generously to all without finding fault, and it will be given to you.

James 1:5 (NIV)

Session 5

He said to them, "Come away by yourselves to a remote place and rest for a while." For many people were coming and going, and they did not even have time to eat.

Mark 6:31 (CSB)

Session 6

I love those who love me; And those who seek me early and diligently will find me.

Proverbs 8:17 (AMP)

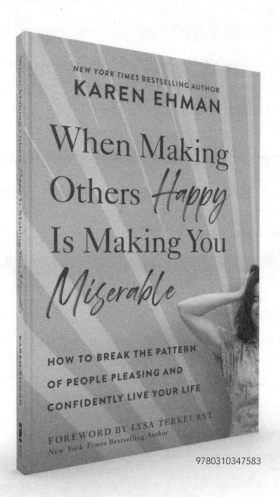

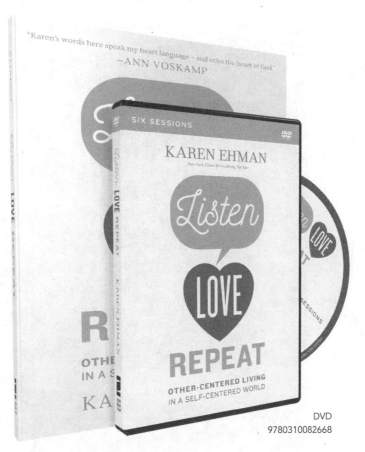

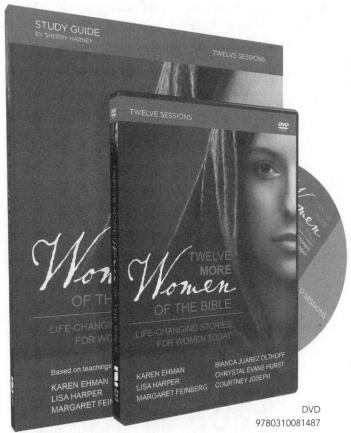

We hope you enjoyed this Bible study from Karen Ehman.
Here are some other Bible studies we think you'll like.

Jennie Allen   Lysa TerKeurst   Megan Fate Marshman   Crystal Evans Hurst

   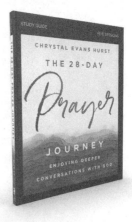

Get Out Of   Forgiving What You   Meant   The 28-Day
Your Head   Can't Forget   For Good   Prayer Journey
Video Study   Video Study   Video Study   Study Guide

───────── OUR MISSION ─────────

Equipping people to understand the Scriptures, cultivate spiritual growth, and live
an inspired faith with Bible study and video resources from today's most trusted voices.

Find your next Bible study, video series, or ministry training at:
HarperChristianResources.com

Proverbs 31
MINISTRIES

Know the Truth. Live the Truth. It changes everything.

If you were inspired by Karen Ehman's *When Making Others Happy Is Making You Miserable* and desire to deepen your own personal relationship with Jesus Christ, Proverbs 31 Ministries has just what you are looking for.

Proverbs 31 Ministries exists to be a trusted friend who will take you by the hand and walk by your side, leading you one step closer to the heart of God through:

- Free online daily devotions
- First 5 Bible study app
- Online Bible studies
- Podcast
- COMPEL writer training
- She Speaks Conference
- Books and resources

Our desire is to help you to know the Truth and live the Truth. Because when you do, it changes everything.

For more information about Proverbs 31 Ministries, visit: www.Proverbs31.org.